The Ultimate Guide to Soccer Positions

Mirsad Hasic

D1114338

DEDICATION

I dedicate this book all soccer players around the world.

CONTENTS

ACKNOWLEDGMENTS

I would like to thank my family for their support.

Introduction

I often receive e-mails from ambitious amateur players asking me things like how to score more goals, how to dribble like a professional, how to dominate in the air, and many other performance-style queries.

A lot of these questions are very broad in nature too, and so would require lots of time explaining things if I were to cover all the angels.

I respond to all the questions I receive, but I do usually have to keep things relatively short because of the sheer number of emails I get at various times, and the subsequent restrictions on my personal time.

Then one day, as I was answering one of these e-mails, it occurred to me that perhaps I should write a book and share everything I know about the eleven soccer positions, from the inside out.

After all, over the years I had noticed a distinct pattern in the types of questions people were asking me, so I had a very good understanding of the kind of things players wanted to know about.

So the mission was on. I made up my mind to run with the idea and compile a comprehensive book on everything I had learned over the years about soccer positions, and I had a lot to share.

I decided also, that I would not share any of the content in this book anywhere on the net. In other words, you will not find any of the text from this book in any other place but this book.

In my "Soccer Positions Guide" I present useful and practical information on all the soccer positions. However, this book is different; in this book you will be able to study each of these positions in a lot more detail.

This ultimate guide gets right down to fundamentals. From the basics, it then works through each position leaving out nothing of any importance. In other words, it's an unabridged version, it's the "ultimate" guide to soccer positions, the only guide you will ever need.

I didn't want to create just another encyclopedia type of book that had an impersonal tone, or a book which was overloaded with masses of unnecessary terminology (there are already plenty of those types of books available online and in the high street).

Instead, I wrote this book with you, my reader, in mind. This meant I had to present the information in a way that amateur players could really relate to. It was important to me not to create something where the reader gets lost in the hype after the first few pages.

There are too many books out there that either focus on generalities or they are written with too much unnecessary detail, resulting in them becoming difficult to follow.

Neither of these types of books ever really gets down to the nitty-gritty side of great soccer techniques, with just enough detail to cover everything properly, and in a style that is truly legible. All the ones I have ever come across fail on both counts.

In this book, however, you will get to learn all about the various soccer positions in detailed yet simplified language. Furthermore, you will also discover chapters on those things which are rarely covered in any detail elsewhere.

Such topics discuss how to read the game, how to avoid unnecessary risk, how to interpret your opponent's next moves, and the real secrets to scoring more goals.

In the beginning you may find some of the details a little bit overwhelming if you're totally new to the game of soccer, and this only to be expected.

My advice to you is to just stick with it and keep reading. Honestly, it won't be too long before you become familiar with the format of the book and the arrangement of its chapters.

Once you become familiar and comfortable with this guide, you will then have real page-tuner in your hands; something that is probably going to keep you awake at night as you enthusiastically absorb everything you can on the first read.

One thing is certain though, and that is you will learn things about soccer positions that you may never have otherwise got to know about.

These are things that you can use to your own advantage as you strive to become that player you have always dreamt of becoming.

While you read through these pages you should try to visualize yourself in real world situations. You are going to use the skills and techniques learned in this book and apply many of them to your own game, first by visualization, and then in real practice situations.

By visualizing first you'll be able to analyze and discover possible pitfalls along the way.

Now that might all sound a bit fanciful to you, but I can guarantee you this: visualization is a tried and tested technique that's been proven to work extremely well in all kinds of situations.

I hope you enjoy reading the "Ultimate Guide to Soccer Positions" as much as I have enjoyed writing it.

Goalie (GK) - The Last Point of Defense

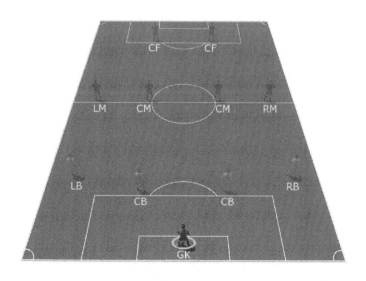

The goalkeeper has one of the most exciting, action-packed positions in soccer. Although goalies are exiled to a small portion of the field, they are still very much involved in the dramas that determine the fate of a game.

Knowing, or not knowing, the secrets behind what makes a great goalkeeper is the difference between winning and losing, a difference needless to say, that can make or break your status on the soccer team.

Here are the seven traits and skills that all of the game's top goalkeepers share.

1. A good goalkeeper knows how to play safely. If you injure yourself repeatedly you will not be a goalie for very long. Knowing how to catch the ball safely, dive safely, and land from jumps safely, is fundamental. You should learn good techniques and then practice them until they become second nature to you. If you do not play safely, then you will never have a chance to build up other essential goalie skills.

2. A good goalkeeper preserves stamina. As a goalie, you will need to put out impressive bursts of action, but save these extreme moves for when they are truly needed. If you exhaust all of your energy reserve in the first 20 minutes or so of a competition, then you are destined to fail.

3. A good goalkeeper uses his entire body to block the ball. Don't just stick out arms and legs and hope it's enough because it won't be. On most occasions you really will need to throw your entire body into the path of an approaching ball. While this may hurt at first, as you get used to it, you will soon learn how to take a hit without suffering too much pain or injury. Putting your full body in the path of a speeding ball obviously creates a larger obstruction. Even if you have misjudged the precise angle and placement of the ball, you are still more likely to make the save when employing your entire body.

4. A good goalkeeper stays totally focused. A soccer ball moves quickly most of the time, so if you take your eyes off it, even for even a few seconds, it may find its way into your goal without you even noticing the shot. World class goalies should always be assessing, not only where the ball is, but where it may be in a few seconds time. You always need to plan ahead if you're to successfully prevent the opposition from scoring. This kind of forward thinking allows you a few extra precious seconds when you need them the most. It also gives a great opportunity for you to position and angle yourself better as the opposition closes in.

5. A good goalkeeper knows how every position on the field is played. Very few players start out as goalies anyway, so most keepers have some firsthand experience of life on the field. Even so, they need to know more than just those positions they have played in themselves. Understanding the strengths and weaknesses of all of the positions allows goalies to predict when and where they need to be to intercept the ball at any given time. It's not enough to just know the basic skills of each position either, but how to execute them yourself. Skills such as passing and dribbling, although not unique to the goalkeeper position, are as important to him as to any other player on the field.

6. A good goalkeeper leads the defense. As a goalie, you have a unique vantage point and can see the field better than any other player on your team. This gives you the opportunity to direct your third of the field to positions and moves that allow your defense to make a coordinated response.

7. A good goalkeeper is fearless. Every goalie can feel a little anxiety when they are crowded, and often become overwhelmed by aggressive forwards, but you can't let this show or affect your decision making. It's important to keep a cool head in all situations. With a bit of practice, a smart goalie can turn himself into the most intimidating player on the field. Being able to give off a kind of menacing aura is something that can actually disrupt goal attempts that are being set up by the opposition. Not only does the goalie have to deal with the forwards from the opposing team, but he may also find himself having to defend his plays sometimes to your own side. While it's all too easy for the field players to blame the keeper for every lost goal, you should not let this stop you from making bold and sometimes risky moves in situations where you think you can pull them off.

Are you now ready to give the challenging and demanding position of goalkeeper a shot now that you understand the fundamentals of what makes a great goalie?

If so, then you are in for the ride of your life. Armed with a little confidence and a few basic skills under your belt, you will soon find yourself developing into the cool, confident goalie that other teams dread.

Ten ways to devastate your game

As every experienced goalkeeper knows, success lies not only in having the right attitude and essential skills, but also the ability to avoid the common pitfalls of this position.

So just what are the snares that seem to catch so many good goalies off guard? Below is a list which outlines the goalkeeper's 10 most common mistakes.

Still, knowing what they are doesn't necessarily help you to avoid them.

Any knowledge without action is pretty futile, so my accompanying avoidance techniques will surely help you to stay out of trouble:

Mistake #1: Being intimidated by the other team.

The Solution: Fear won't accomplish anything but it will affect your ability to think and play well.

Instead of focusing directly on your opponents, concentrate on what they are about to do, or trying to do, and think of how you will respond to that.

Even the most formidable forward will have problems getting a ball past an alert, skilled goalkeeper.

Mistake #2: Waiting for your opponent.

The Solution: If an opponent is approaching you then you should be approaching him as well. Straighten up and put your elbows out to make yourself as large as possible, and then begin to move in on the ball.

This will not only make it physically harder to get the ball around you, but it will intimidate your opponent and make it more difficult for him to think quickly and clearly.

Mistake #3: Kicking or throwing the ball without forethought.

The Solution: Always have a plan of action. Analyze the situation and know exactly what end your move is going to accomplish. Keep mindful of questions like where is the ball going? Who will take possession of it next?

Will you be defending your goal again in a few moments? This split second thinking can make all the difference to the outcome of an attack and consequently the game.

Mistake #4: Ignoring or denying your weaknesses.

The Solution: The only way to fix a problem is to acknowledge it for what it is, and then make a plan to overcome it.

You won't be the first goalkeeper to display flaws; on the contrary, all soccer players have some shortcomings.

The difference between a professional player and an average amateur is the willingness to seek out every weak point and work on it until it finally becomes a strength. If you are having a hard time assessing your own performance, ask your coach for guidance.

Mistake #5: Thinking inside the box.

The Solution: Come out of the goal box when the situation warrants it. Staying back in the goal makes you look smaller and less powerful, plus it will result in you becoming a ball catcher instead of a fully-fledged goalkeeper.

Coming toward your opponents will have two positive effects. First it will make it harder to get the ball past you, and second, it will force opponents to make a move before they are ready to.

Mistake #6: Spending all of your time and energy on a few key players.

The solution: While it's important to identify and watch the best opposing strikers, focusing exclusively on one or two players will leave you and your goal wide open. Watch the star strikers yes, but keep an eye on everyone else as well.

Mistake #7: Holding back in practice.

The Solution: Give it your all at practice, and let no skill go unlearned. Many goalies assume that because of their position they are above basic skills such as dribbling, when in fact nothing could be farther from the truth.

Do drills with the rest of your team and don't let any part of your game get rusty. You'll regret it if you do!

Mistake #8: Having unattainable goals.

The Solution: Set realistic goals for your self-improvement. While it's good to challenge yourself, expecting perfection, for example, is an unrealistic, unattainable target, which will only result in frustration and even a possible setback to your development.

Always aim for good progress, not perfection, and you will improve just fine.

Mistake #9: Taking unnecessary risks.

The Solution: Learn good form and practice it until you do it out of habit. Too many potentially great goalies end up quitting the position or even the game of soccer completely by letting themselves down.

This is all because they took too many risks too often that were way too ambitious and far too unnecessary. In other words, they gambled against all the odds and lost.

The consequence of this type of behavior often results in bitter disappointment at best and permanent injury at worse. It's important to know you limitations!

Mistake #10: Giving 90% or less.

The Solution: Your team deserves every ounce of energy, skill, and mojo you can summon. Play every game like it was a cup final, as if your life depended on it.

Don't treat any game as just as a friendly kick-around with mates, even if that's what it is. NEVER lose your winning spirit.

Ten easy steps to becoming a great goalie

Many people think that the position of goalkeeper is just too complicated and too stressful to master well, and it should therefore be reserved for a certain type of individual who is best matched for the role.

Well, nothing could be further from the truth. Any fit and able player can adapt to becoming a good goalie, providing that is, he is 100% dedicated and totally focused.

There are a few common practices and habits that, when adhered to, can make all the difference to a goalkeeper's success. By learning these 10 simple "dos", you too can become a respected goalie if you want to.

1. **Do** stay fit. It's easy to let yourself go as a goalie if you're not careful. After all, when compared to the 10 field players, you are spending more time waiting around than you are running around. Even so, fitness is just as important to a goalkeeper as it is to any other team player. Goalies do most of their work in short bursts, but these short bursts will be compromised if the goalkeeper doesn't make a concerted effort to stay in good physical shape.

2. **Do** participate in all drills. Make sure you participate in every training session; even the ones you don't think apply to your role as a goalie. Goalkeepers who ignore basics will live to regret it.

3. **Do** develop a good goalkeeper stance and maintain it in both practice and games. Goalkeepers should not stand perfectly upright because this is not a good starting position for the dives and other quick movements that the job requires. Instead, goalies should keep their knees bent and stand on the balls of their feet, keeping them at about shoulder width apart. What this stance does is allow you to respond quickly with movements in either direction, and also to shift your weight around effectively. The more you bend your knees, the greater your ability becomes to respond rapidly to low or a high flying balls.

4. **Do** watch professional soccer. Study professional goalkeepers and the way they defend their goals. Take note of their strengths, skills, and intuition, and see if you can adopt and adapt any of what you learn into your own unique style of play.

5. **Do** learn how to use your hands to catch a ball without hurting or injuring yourself. As a goalie, you will be the only player who spends a lot of time with his hands on the ball. It's important that you use this privilege to your best advantage. More important still is learning how to catch a ball properly. This is typically done by using holds such as the Heart and the W. These unique methods of catching the ball help to prevent broken fingers and other injuries to the hands and wrists. In short, there's more to catching a ball than just catching a ball!

6. **Do** catch the ball with your body instead of your limbs. After catching the ball you should immediately pull it in toward your torso. This absorbs some of the shock of the catch and also stabilizes the ball. By catching in this way you also get to use a wider area of your body for blocking. All of these things combined are tactics that contribute toward your success when saving shots fired at your goal.

7. **Do** become an expert on goal kicks and throws. These two skills can make or break your game depending on how well you manage them. Kicks and throws determine where the ball goes to next and who takes it from there. No other players in soccer have this privilege with the ball, so don't let the chance go to waste.

8. **Do** watch for angles from where the opposing team can attempt shots at your goal. You don't want to wear out your cleats by endlessly chasing balls around the goal area, so learn to play smart rather than hard. Because very few players will kick the ball where a score is highly improbable, angling yourself correctly can discourage them and save your precious stamina by reducing the attacks on your goal.

9. **Do** be intimidating (without breaking rules, of course). It's okay (and sometimes completely necessary) to be and to look aggressive while defending your territory.

10. **Do** tell your teammates how best to support you. Quite often a goalie can see plays before they even happen. You will also be the first person to see the team changing strategies, and therefore the perfect person to direct the defense accordingly. Don't be afraid to direct your defense to the positions where they can best help you. Everyone has a common purpose here, and that is to win the game. Teamwork is the key.

Diving without risking your life

The goalie's job will often take you a lot closer to the ground than you would like to be. It's the nature of the position.

A great goalkeeper does everything he can do to stop that ball passing his goal line. This typically involves leaping, diving, and sliding for balls from any angle, and in all weathers.

This commitment and dedication to the position can, and on occasion does, have a very negative side to it with regards to injury risk.

More often than not, a goalkeeper's injuries will cause little more than a temporary setback, but other times, injuries may prove to be more severe and lasting.

Goalkeeping is, in fact, quite a vulnerable position. Playing as goalkeeper is a great job and really rewarding for those who are passionate about it, but it's definitely not a position for the faint-hearted.

The kinds of injuries that are common with diving incidents include bruises and scrapes mostly, and in most cases are unavoidable.

However, goalkeepers are more exposed to a few other serious types of injury than field players are.

Some of these may include broken bones, serious strains, sprains, and even head injuries.

A lot of these types of injury are caused by diving incorrectly, and that means they could have been avoided.

It's not difficult to get hurt and injured when you're throwing yourself around in an attempt to block the ball, but it's very important to be as safe as possible while you're doing it.

That means you need to avoid putting yourself in harm's way when it's really not necessary.

Below is a simple plan for diving safely, and by safely, that simply means without risking life and limb in the process.

The first rule to be mindful of is to set up the dive properly. Many goalies find that the best way to do this is to turn out their "diving side" leg and keep its foot squarely on the ground until it's time to take off.

You should then use the other leg to pivot and position yourself comfortably. What this position does is enable you to be more acrobatic, which not only allows you to reach the ball faster, but it also gives you better control over the actual dive.

Once you're in the right position, you are then well prepared for saving the ball. You then extend your body to receive the ball, and then immediately tuck yourself in once you have it in your possession.

So the moment you get the ball in your hands, you pull it into your abdominal region and instantly tuck your arms and elbows in to the sides.

Any limbs that are sticking out when you land will receive more than their fair share of force. This hard impact is what can lead to injuries and breaks if you're not careful.

Therefore, always try to land in the safest possible position and practice regularly in between games. Avoid landing on your stomach or back at all costs.

Hard landings on your front or back can result in internal damage, and broken ribs are a very real possibility.

The ideal way to land from a dive is on your sides, with the ball held tight to your stomach and the shoulders properly hunched in. Keep a picture of the perfect dive in your mind so that it becomes hardwired.

When diving and landing properly, it is your elbows that will receive most of the impact. Many goalkeepers find that rolling slightly as they hit the ground allows them to dissipate a lot of the force from the impact.

This style of landing further cuts down the potential for bruising and injuries.

Do not ever dive with your head first. Always dive from the side and keep your head out of the path of the ball, and more importantly, the path of the player's boots.

If you dive with your head first, then there's a good chance that you could land on your stomach or even your face, as well as having your opponents accidentally strike your head as they go for the ball.

These are all unnecessary dangers that carry a high risk of injury.

Diving with your head first also takes away your control as it prevents you from watching the ball. The safest way to play is to always stay focused on the ball and plan your dives quickly, and with safety in mind.

This is a far better approach than just throwing yourself into the path of the ball willy-nilly, hoping against hope for a safe and successful outcome.

The golden rule here is to dive only when it is necessary and don't dive when it's not. There is a huge difference to an outcome when taking a calculated risk as opposed to taking unnecessary risks, the latter being not only dangerous but quite probably unsuccessful too.

Although diving for the ball can be dramatic, impressive, and entertaining for those watching the game, it also carries with it a higher risk of injury compared to other methods of saving like catching, jumping, and sliding.

Never dive when another move will have the same result and a lower risk of harm.

To summarize this chapter: Goalies have a higher injury rate than field players, but many of these injuries are totally unnecessary.

Knowing when to take more extreme measures to save the ball, and how to perform these with minimal risk, will help protect you and allow you to play the position of goalie for years to come.

Knowing when to jump for the ball

To jump or not to jump, that is the question for many novice and experienced goalkeepers alike. The ability to jump effectively is an absolute "must have" skill for any successful goalkeeper.

Leaping for the ball allows you to save high shots and also move quickly from one area to another.

However, many goalkeepers misuse their jumping ability to show off with. It can be quite dramatic at times, and therefore become a real attention grabber and crowd pleaser.

But playing in goal is not an audition for a circus act. A goalie should always save the ball using the most effective and safe option available to him, even if it's just a straightforward, unentertaining catch.

How then, do goalkeepers know when to jump and when to keep their feet firmly planted on the ground?

Well, many goalies assume that they should jump whenever in doubt, but the most successful veteran goalkeepers know that a very different approach is usually best.

Before leaping for any ball, you should assess whether you can reach it from the center area. The best option is always when you can get to a ball without using extreme measures.

Again, your job is not to entertain onlookers, but to save goals, although the former is inevitable when great saves are made.

There will always be occasions where you get to display your acrobatic skills for difficult saves, so try not to create them out of nothing when it really isn't necessary. Save you energy so that you have it when you most need it.

The strategy behind successful jumps is to use good common sense, and to always keep safety in the forefront of your mind at all times. There should never be any compromise on your well-being.

So when you decide to jump for the ball, you should also know how and where you expect to land from that jump.

Deciding when to jump is not a difficult decision, or at least it shouldn't be for anyone who's been playing in goal for a while.

The answer is to only jump for the ball when jumping is the only way to save it, and when you are reasonably sure you can execute the move safely. That's it, in a nutshell.

When not to jump for the ball is a decision that needs to be made quickly based on a number of factors. There are in fact several good reasons to avoid making unnecessary jumps.

Because a jump usually takes you far from the center, it may actually create an opening for the opposing team to score in cases where you have misjudged their intention.

Similarly, because landing and recovering from a jump can take a while, you will be out of play momentarily after the jump, thus opening up a potential window of opportunity for your opponents.

Another negative side to jumping is that injuries are common, mainly from bad landings. Every time you jump, you are taking a risk that may not end as you had planned it to.

One of the reasons why a lot of goalkeepers make a jump when it's not really necessary is because they get caught up in the moment.

When adrenaline kicks in, they just go for the save, almost on autopilot. In situations like these, instinct and panic takes the place of rational thinking, quite often to the detriment of the keeper.

At other times, a goalkeeper would sooner take action than not take action, even when he knows a jumping attempt to save the ball has little or no chance of succeeding.

After all, standing idly by as a shot heads toward his goal is not going to win him any popularity contests, and popularity within a soccer team is important to a lot of players, or at least having the respect of the team is.

So doing nothing, as opposed to doing something, no matter how futile, is always the better option in the mind of a goalie.

Lastly, many goalkeepers, and soccer players more generally, tend to enjoy a bit of showing off whenever an opportunity presents itself.

Making bold moves to showcase their skills is certain to bring the kind of attention from onlookers that these players relish. So to some, these opportunities to shine become irresistible, even if their little displays contribute nothing to the outcome of the game.

Performing competent jumps with safe landings is an essential skill for goalkeepers, but knowing when to, and when not to jump, is equally as important.

Keeping a cool head and being able to make informed decisions will always increase the chance of a successful save.

Experience, knowledge, and taking the right actions based on these attributes, is something which will help any goalie to become someone who is both feared and respected by his opponents.

Interpreting your opponent's next move

There are many advantages to being able to interpret your opponent's next move. Firstly, it gives you time to contemplate your next move, and therefore time to position yourself for the best response.

Secondly, it allows you to influence the outcome of the game by making moves that might have been impossible if you had allowed the situation to take you by surprise.

While all soccer players would agree that interpreting an opponent's next move is incredibly useful, field players don't generally have as much opportunity to do this as their goalkeeper.

This is because the goalkeeper has a unique position on the field, a place from where he can spot and react to the opposing team's plays a lot quicker than any of the other players.

A goalkeeper who has a good grip on interpreting his opponents next moves can singlehandedly save a game and emerge as a team leader.

However, this skill, like all other skills, takes practice, and is one which can only improve with experience. And also like any other skill, there are some who become really good at it, whereas others find it a lot harder.

I've listed a few pointers below that will definitely give you a good foundation on which to build this special skill. It is then up to you to develop this talent and take your goalkeeping abilities up to a whole new level.

How to interpret your opponent's next moves:

- *Develop your intuition by predicting possible situations and preparing for them.* To begin with, just keep going through the motions and eventually you will start seeing positive results as you gain more experience. After you do this, it's important to assess the outcome based on your decisions and try to understand where you went right or wrong. The best goalies have developed very good intuition over time, and the only way they were able to acquire this vital skill was to begin making predictions. Their ability to improve came about purely by trial, error, and learning from any wrong assumptions along the way.

- *Keep your eyes low.* While it's easy for an opponent to fake intention with their body and eye movements, it's more difficult for them to set up a pass or other move without showing their intentions in their feet, or more specifically, the supporting foot. The direction that this foot points to is often the direction that the player intends to shoot. Another advantage of watching your opponents' feet is that the ground is usually where the ball is, which you should never lose sight of anyway.

- *Pay special attention to diagonal movement.* While it's normal for a player to constantly change direction on a field, what's particularly useful to know is that whenever he moves diagonally he is most likely positioning himself for a play. Take notice of these people and be prepared for them to take possession of the ball very soon. There can be very few surprise scores when you are well prepared.
- *Pay attention to chatter.* Some teams play a quiet, straightforward game, while others like to talk, or scream and shout, or both. Sometimes these noisy players are trying to lead the opposing team astray by tricking then into thinking they're about to make certain moves that they have no actual intention of making. These types of players should be easy to pick out at the beginning of the game. Other times, opposing players may try to verbally taunt and intimidate you. The reason behind this unfair tactic is to distract you and therefore impair your ability to save. Either way, knowing how the rival team operates can help you predict their next moves.
- *Watch the other player's as well.* A common goalie mistake is to focus almost exclusively on the opponents most likely to attempt a shot at his goal. While it's important to pay special attention to these players, it's also important to be aware of the other players on the field too. You never know when a "less than stellar" player is going to appear out of nowhere and attempt to put the ball into your net.

Honing in on these skills will give you time to think of your own strategy and put you in a good position to carry it through successfully.

Knowing how to monitor your opponents and interpret their next moves is the key to successful goalkeeping.

This vital skill allows you to act quickly and intelligently. It means you will be in a good position to make better informed decisions at the time, thus helping you to counter the opponent's strategies and help lead your team to victory.

So You Want to Be a Defender

Are you interested in the position of defender but can't quite decide if it's the right one for you or not? If so, there are a few easy ways to tell.

What you are about to read might seem a little overwhelming or discouraging to begin with, but try not to be put off by the details.

Although the attributes required for a defender position could be summarized in a single paragraph, it's important to read the necessary requirements in a little more detail.

This will help you to better ascertain whether it's a position you could apply for now, or, one in which you could develop your skills for first, and then apply for at a later date.

The first thing you need to know about the defender position is that it's one where thinking quickly and logically is fundamental to the role.

A good defender can soon assess the strengths and weaknesses of his opponents.

Once he's done this he's able to develop a plan of action that allows him to exploit any weaknesses that he's picked up on.

This in turn should mess with any of their strong point as a consequence. Good defenders are experts at deductive reasoning.

Another key trait of a good defender is his ability to strategize. They are good at reading the game overall, and predicting moves of the opposing side.

As a defender, you should be able to overcome even the fastest or most skilled offense through quick and decisive thinking. Similarly, you should be able to analyze your own performance on the field and adapt it to the game being played.

It's also important that you learn from your own mistakes and move on quickly to a more appropriate plan B, whenever a situation warrants it.

Everyone makes mistakes, but it takes a real star to openly admit to them and learn something useful from his blunders.

A defender's strengths are obviously not limited to the use of his brain. If you want to be a good defender then you will need to be one of the most physically fit players on the field too.

Not only must you be fast enough and strong enough to face down any challenging opponents, but you must also have the stamina to do this for the entire duration of a game.

In order to win competitions, a team's defenders must end with the same fast reflexes and superior energy that they started with, or very near to it.

Teamwork is another essential trait of a good defender. Defense is one area of the field where no maverick is going to win the game without the support of his teammates.

Not only do you need to be able to direct your team to the positions where they can best support you, but you also have to take their directions and support them back when needs arise.

The defensive team must have a high level of trust, respect, and cooperation in order to successfully defend their goal and win the game.

As a defender, you need to have some of the best technical skills on the team. You should be well rounded and able to mark or tackle an opponent and succeed in duels.

Superior ball skills are also a must-have quality, so be sure to practice basics such as heading, dribbling and passing, and maintain any skills that you have previously mastered, including those which you don't get to use all that often.

You should be experienced in using your skills in a variety of situations, both in practice and when in the midst of the most intense games.

Finally, even if you're not the perfect candidate for a defender position right now, then that shouldn't be any reason to stop you from becoming the perfect candidate further down the line.

The best defenders are often the most experienced and dedicated and they have an unwavering determination to succeed. They are not necessarily the ones who began their soccer career with the most talent.

If this is a position that appeals to you personally, then you need to start working on strategy, teamwork, technical skills, and all of the other things needed to become an awesome defender.

Centre Back (CB) - The Heart of Defense

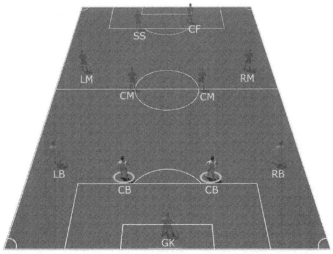

Centre backs, also called central defenders, form the core of a soccer team's defense. They are strong, fast players, with superb intuition and an uncanny ability to be in the right place at the right time.

Key duties

The key duty of a centre back is to defend the goal, first and foremost. As such, good tackling skills are an absolute must-have, especially intercepting and blocking.

Being able to play offensively is a good trait to have in any player, but in the position of centre back this should take a back seat to defensive strategy.

A centre back is the counter to the opposing team's centre forward, so those in this position need to be physically and emotionally strong, and have the mental gumption to face down players and take the ball with confidence.

Because they play as part of a team, and therefore often take direction from the goalie, a high level of teamwork and cooperation is yet another vital skill.

Essential traits

One of the key traits of a centre back is good communication. Defensive players must cover a relatively large area of the field and keep track of the movements of several opposing players.

In order to spread the work evenly and ensure that there are no "holes" in the defense, centre backs, along with other defensive players, must be good at communicating with their teammates.

Awareness is another quality that is very beneficial to a centre back. People often talk about the intuitiveness of this position, but this is actually a byproduct of being very aware of one's surroundings.

Good centre backs are the first players to see a strategy unfolding in the other team's offense, or to notice and fill a deficiency in their own team's defensive line.

While centre backs of the past tended to be strong, rather than fast, this has changed in modern day soccer. A twenty-first century centre back is usually a very fast player.

He prefers to use his superior speed to take the ball rather than challenging opponents head-on. Even so, having reasonable strength is still an important trait of a centre back because he will be up against strong center forwards.

Height is another consideration, and although this is not absolutely essential to the role, most talented centre backs do tend to be on the tall side.

Being tall obviously makes it easier to intercept high crosses. Height is also an advantage when going up against the opposing team's centre forwards, who also tend to be tall.

Finally, centre backs need to have solid technical skills, especially tackling, heading and ball control.

Although it's important to be strong in all the major soccer and ball handling skills, the three mentioned above will be called upon in every single game you play as a centre back.

Drawbacks

There are a few drawbacks to the position of centre back, not least because there are so many demands that it's easy to become distracted.

You also need to be aware of the boundaries of this position.

While it's wonderful to take the ball all the way to the goal whenever you have the opportunity, you always need to make sure your own position is covered.

The ideal centre back

The ideal centre back is tall, fast, and strong. More importantly is that he's mentally strong and not afraid to face down intimidating opponents in challenging situations.

Good centre backs have solid technical skills too, plus a fast intellect that allows them to adapt their skills to best effect in the quickest possible time.

If you think you have what it takes to fulfill this important position on your team, then it may be time to give it a shot and see how you fare.

With a lot of practice, and oodles of determination, you may find that you are the perfect person for this challenging role.

Don't take unnecessary risks

Centre backs are truly central to the success or failure of soccer games. They play a vital role in the defense and must have superior skills as well an unshakable self-confidence.

However, having an unshakable self-confidence shouldn't mean you are fearless to the point where anything goes regardless of the consequences, yet that is exactly what happens at times, with some of them.

Indeed, one of the common mistakes of the centre back position is taking unnecessary risks and making rash decisions that end up jeopardizing the entire game.

A typical and totally unnecessary risk taken by defenders in general, and centre backs in particular, is to "push up" toward the centre line.

Although there are some advantages for spreading out the defensive players, the downside is that it will often leave only minimal support for the goalkeeper.

In many formations, a better choice is to stay deep in the defensive third.

This makes it difficult for the opposing team's forwards to make any headway, and almost impossible for them to make a score.

Another common and unnecessary risk is committing too early to a play or some other course of action. Some types of tackles, and various other physical plays, require time to recover and regroup.

Therefore, it's never a good idea to attempt one of these unless you are certain that it can be pulled off successfully.

It is not so uncommon to see a centre back tricked into committing to a move, only for him to then be left standing there dusting himself off as the opponent runs away with the ball. This doesn't have to happen to you providing you have your game in order.

Playing without knowing the likely outcome is a risk that is almost always unnecessary, and one which often ends in a failed attempt.

Many centre backs are often too quick to jump into heading duels; yet another unnecessary risk. It is no good being the one whose forehead contacts the ball first if you have no plan to follow through with after that contact.

If you head the ball without knowing which direction or which player to head it to, then you haven't really won that duel at all.

Another unnecessary risk is the long-shot pass. If there is only a small probability of such a pass reaching its destination without being intercepted by the opposition, then you should find another solution, such as dribbling or finding a teammate closer by who is more likely to receive your pass and then do something useful with the ball after he gets possession of it.

Making a pass that is probably going to get blocked as it travels from A-B, is like handing the soccer ball directly to your opponents.

It's okay to have a quick think before making these types of risky moves, especially when a little pause for thought could result in a much better defense for your team.

The definition of an unnecessary risk changes from team to team, and even from situation to situation.

If you have the speed, reflexes and sharp wit needed to recover from a play, then something may not be as much of a risk as it might be for another, slower player. In other words, the risk element is often relative to the individual and the individual situation.

If your team is good at winning back lost balls, then you may not have to worry as strenuously about the exact direction of it when it leaves your head or foot.

It's important to assess every situation individually and try to make informed decisions as best you can. Just remember, all decisions have consequences.

Every defensive action holds a certain amount of risk, so try not to add to these by gambling unnecessarily.

Furthermore, going all out with both guns blazing at every opportunity, not only increases the chance of a blunder on the field, but you also risk using up your limited energy supplies, or worse still, injuring yourself.

Reading the game and showing discretion are two traits that set truly great soccer players apart from the rest.

Knowing when to take a risk and when to play it safe can make all the difference in the quality of your overall game.

Thinking with your head is just as important as thinking with your feet.

Heading duels

Although most soccer teams aim to play a neat and well-organized game, and attempt to keep the ball on or low to the ground as much as possible, heading will always be an inevitable part of any competition, whether you like it or not.

Winning headers, be that defensively or offensively, is one of the most important aspects of a soccer game, especially one which is high tempo. The outcome of any heading duel can also influence on the outcome of a game.

Even though all players must compete for an aerial ball whenever it's required of them, it is the ones who play the position of centre-back whose heading-skills are most often put to the test.

Possessing excellent aerial skills are necessary for anyone who plays, or wants to play, as a central defender.

Two good examples of having excellent aerial ability are John Terry (the captain of Chelsea) and Carles Puyol (former Barcelona defender).

These guys have demonstrated countless times through their skills how to successfully defend high balls that come from crosses, corners and free kicks.

Be mindful that any weakness or minor mistake in the air can produce a terrible outcome for the team, the most obvious of which is conceding a goal.

It is essential that centre-backs work tirelessly and constantly to improve and maintain this aspect of their game.

As a centre-back, your heading-skills can mean the difference between you being a good defender or a truly-great defender, that's how important aerial play is to your game.

Below are five pointers that will help you to improve your heading capability.

1. *Keep your eyes on the ball at all times during a game*: At any moment a ball could be in full flight and heading in your direction. When a high ball does find its way over to you, ready yourself by determining the ball's line-of-flight. You then need to position yourself under the ball while at the same time allowing for a few steps back. This is so that you can get a run at the ball just when it's needed. Remember to keep the ball in your sight constantly, and try to stay ahead of the opponents, or at least plan to position yourself in front of them just at the right moment.

2. *A key element to good heading is timing.* Having positioned yourself correctly, time your run at the ball so that you can connect with it just at the right moment and with maximum power. Use the momentum from your forward surge to achieve a higher jump and a more solid attack.

3. *The Jump.* Keep your elbows and arms out. This will help you to maintain balance and power, and also keeps your opponent at a distance. Be careful with your arms though. Raising them too high or too aggressively could result in a foul.

4. *Keep your eyes fixed on the ball right up until the point of impact.* Monitoring the ball closely will help you to better control the direction you want to send it in, which is hopefully at the feet of one of your teammates. Wherever possible, use your lower-forehead (just above the eyes) to connect with the ball. This allows you greater control as well as reduces the potential for injury.

5. *Remember to implement correct positioning and body-form.* It's important that you know how to position yourself correctly and prepare your body for the header. These fundamentals will help you to avoid injury and achieve the primary objective of your aerial duel, which is to succeed. This really is only something that can be developed by plenty of practice and practical experience. Providing you do practice hard, it won't be too long before you intuitively have positioning, preparation, and timing down to a fine art.

As with any skill, you must run through heading scenarios over and over until everything finally clicks together.

Even when you get good at headings, there is no time to rest on your laurels. This, just other skills, has to be maintained and developed still further after it's been mastered.

That means practice never stops, although it will become less intense compared to learning from scratch.

A useful and very simple training set-up is to have a teammate or a friend throw or kick balls at you from different angles and heights.

Keep this type of training up and your aerial skills will definitely become stronger. Your chief objective here is to dominate heading duels on the field.

Safe and legal tackles

As a center back, you are in a unique position.

While most other positions are focused on moving the ball, your primary goal is to stop the opposing team players from advancing forward in any way you can. Although center backs occasionally get to score goals themselves, goal scoring is not actually their main purpose.

The role of a center back is defined by his ability to effectively block opponent's attempts to push through the defense and shoot at the goal.

One of the most effective ways to stop opponents from advancing is by tackling, although tackling per se has become something of a touchy subject in modern soccer.

There has even been a movement to ban certain types of tackle, such as challenging from behind, as one example. Many centre backs actually avoid tackling altogether because it's become so easy to get a yellow or even a red card.

Centre backs now tend to focus more on intercepting the ball, something that has not traditionally been their main approach.

Despite all the drawbacks, tackling is still a vital skill. Knowing how to tackle legally and safely can give you an incredible edge over your opponents.

Below are three different types of effective tackle, all of which are perfectly legal in the game of soccer:

1. *The block tackle*: This is a great centre back technique because no one gets hurt and the ball changes possession quickly. It is best used when opponents are coming straight toward you. As they approach, you get squarely in their path. You need to keep both legs out with your weight evenly distributed so that you can shift your weight quickly when needed. As the ball approaches, extend the leg closest to the ball and allow the inside of your foot to change its direction. It is important that you keep your leg firm, using a great deal of muscle tension, as this prevents both injury and being knocked off your feet.

2. *The poke tackle*: In a poke tackle you will approach your opponent from the side or from behind. You will need to quickly discern where the player is heading and then keep closely behind him. When the moment is right, simply extend your leg either around the player or through his legs, and then just tap the ball away. Because you will recover quickly from this approach, you can then take possession of the ball and do something useful with it. Whatever you do, make sure you only make contact with the ball and not the opponent. Physical contact with the opponent will most likely have the referee calling a foul.

3. *The sliding tackle*: This is a dramatic move that involves throwing yourself to the ground and sliding across the grass in your pursuit of the ball. It is one of the more effective forms of tackling because of its speed and surprise element. However, the sliding tackle must be executed correctly to prevent injury and penalties. The first thing to be mindful of is that the grass needs to be thick and at least damp, if not truly wet. On dry or thin grass you will fall hard and stop suddenly, as opposed to sliding. Obviously an attempted slide tackle on the wrong kind of surface can result in a possible injury too. The second point to note is to keep the tackling foot low, on the ground. If it is raised then you may inadvertently strike your opponent. Under the newest regulations, an ineffective slide tackle can earn at least a yellow card, so this is a move that is best reserved for a "can't miss" moment.

40 yard crosses

A 40-yard cross can be a make or break moment in your game. If the cross is successful, morale will skyrocket and you will become an instant star.

If a 40-yard cross fails, however, as some inevitably do, then your teammates may blame you for taking unnecessary risks.

Only experience will help you to make the best informed choices in these situations.

You must never be afraid to make a 40-yard cross when a situation warrants it.

This is an ability that every centre back must have in his skills arsenal. When executed well, a 40-yard cross field pass is something that really does help to keep the team confidence high and the players enthused.

Although these long passes do have the potential to change the course of a game, many players skip 40-yard crosses, and other long passes, when they are training.

This can come at a great cost to the side. Knowing how to execute these field passes accurately can "wow" teammates while intimidating opponents at the same time, especially when the outcome turns out exactly how you had planned it to.

Being able to perform these long passes confidently can also get you out of tight situations whenever the opposing team is moving in and there are no teammates nearby to pass the ball to.

Below are a few tips to help you decide when to perform a 40-yard cross and how to be as accurate as possible when executing it.

- *Be safe*: Don't even try a 40-yard cross if you have two or more unmarked teammates nearby. If it misses (and there's always a potential for that), then you will have to explain to some very annoyed teammates why you decided to take the chance.

- *Know when to keep the ball*: Only try a long shot when you are in immediate danger of losing the ball to an opponent, or, the situation is one where a long pass looks like it could result in a very favorable outcome. Otherwise, keep the ball in your possession or pass it to a nearby teammate who is in a better position than you to do something useful with it. In short, don't take unnecessary risks just because you can.
- *Know that your teammates are ready*: Ideally, this means they are watching the ball intently and are unmarked, or they are able to lose their opponents relatively easily when the moment comes.
- *Follow through*: Your job is not over the moment the ball leaves your feet. You should immediately mark any opponent near you to keep him from moving in on the teammate who now possesses the ball, or is about to possess it. Until your teammate has trapped the ball and got it under his control, you are still responsible for its safety.

As with all soccer skills, no one is born knowing just how and when to execute this pass with total certainty.

It takes a lot of practice and a healthy dose of game intuition before anyone can become the master of long passes.

All the same, the 40-yard cross-field pass is a skill that's well worth learning and honing in on.

Once you have mastered it - *by 'mastering' that means knowing the unique circumstances when you can safely execute it, and not just being able to physically perform the pass* - then you will have yet another very useful weapon in your passing skills arsenal.

Sweeper (SW) – The Soccer Field Maestro

The position of sweeper, or libero as it's often referred to, is one of the most versatile in soccer, and also one of the most specialized.

Although sweepers play primarily in the relatively small patch of soccer real estate, the area immediately in front of the goal, they are also known to carry the ball forward and give support to other defenders and midfielders whenever necessary.

If you are a sweeper, then you are one of the most gifted and multi-talented members of your team.

Furthermore, you are free to use your skills to the team's best advantage in a whole variety of different situations.

The role of a sweeper

Positioned just meters from their own goal, sweepers are the last line of defense against the opposing team's offense.

Because sweepers are not generally responsible for marking opponents, tackling, or any of the other traditional defensive duties, it leaves them free to exclusively defend the goal.

This relative freedom of theirs is why the position is often referred to as "libero", which simply means "to set free" in Latin.

Every sweeper has a distinctive style that meshes with his unique gifts and skills. Some prefer to stay back, remaining in front of the goal box at all times.

This limits their play to only those moments where the ball has broken through the defense. Others play the ball forward on the field and even back up midfielders.

There are definite benefits and drawbacks to both styles of play, and different variations work best for the different teams and the individual sweepers.

There are, however, a few restrictions on the freedom of this position.

Although the sweeper can play immediately in front of the box, or leave his area to support other positions, he generally doesn't venture far into the flanks of the field.

When all's said and done, a team is depending on their sweeper to defend the goal, so he cannot venture too far from it too often.

Benefits and drawbacks

As already mentioned, the obvious benefit of the sweeper position is the freedom that it entails. You are literally free to go wherever your team most needs you. However, this can present a "catch 22" of sorts.

If you venture too far from the goal box, then you leave your assigned area wide open, and that kind of defeats the purpose of your role to protect the goal.

If you stay deep in the defense, you may feel that you are spending much of your time watching the game instead of playing in it.

This may cause frustration at times, especially in situations where you believe your help might have been useful if you were deployed somewhere else.

Sometimes the freedom can be a detriment because you, as a sweeper, must define your own role on the team.

Necessary skills

A sweeper must often come up with strategies that they alone can carry out.

The stakes are high by the time the ball gets to the sweeper's patch, often with a goal for the opposing team looking imminent if no immediate action is taken. The pressure is certainly on at this phase of play.

When opponents are invading the sweeper's domain, his number one obligation is to use his ability to read the situation, predict what will happen next, and then make plans for every contingency. This all has to be decided within seconds.

Because a sweeper will usually be executing his plans without the assistance of the other players, and under great pressure from the opposing team too, he therefore has to demonstrate superior ball skills.

His primary concern will be to get the ball away from the goal area as quickly as possible, and to do this he needs to be able to pass quickly and with great accuracy if his defensive action is to be successful.

Intercepting the ball is another key skill that you need to have if you want to become a successful sweeper.

You must take possession of the ball and move it immediately and safely to other players on your team. Interceptions play a large role in a sweeper's obligations, as do other skills such as tackling.

Personality traits

Not only must you be a fast thinker and good strategist to play in the position of sweeper, but you must be calm and very confident in your abilities as well.

Most of your moves will be performed under extreme pressure, first physical pressure from the opposing team, and second, mental pressure caused by the need to think quickly and act on those thoughts.

What you do and how quickly you do it determines the outcome of your actions.

You must be assertive enough to take the ball from opponents and gutsy enough to pass it through a seeming throng of forwards.

If you think you have what it takes to be a sweeper, then it's time to act and see if you can secure yourself a trial position on your team.

OK, so here's a recap of the prerequisites you will need to have, or are willing to develop, for the sweeper position.

You need to demonstrate superior ball skills in all areas. You also need to have a strong mind and possess both the ability and the courage to act on your thoughts quickly and without any hesitation.

So if you find yourself longing for the freedom to play the game without too many restrictions, then this may be the perfect position for you.

Just remember though, that freedom comes with a whole lot of responsibility and accountability.

Good fitness

No other defensive player is quite as important to a soccer team as a sweeper, and few players have the same physical demands.

Sweepers must defend their team's goal like their life depends on it. They often need to follow up with their own offensive players as well.

Although the sweeper does not have to run up and down the field like some of the other players do, he still has to perform intense bursts of energy; out-thinking and out-running all the opposing team's offense.

The only way for you to get yourself into prime sweeper condition is to devote a part of the day, most days, for exercise and training.

You will only get out what you put in, and the sweeper position requires that you put in a lot of skill, energy, and true grit at all times, so you might want to bear that in mind when preparing your practice sessions.

Below are some of the essential areas where sweepers must excel in physical fitness levels, along with some suggestions for exercises that will help you to develop in these areas:

1. *Sprinting over a short distance*: Although sweepers don't run long distances on a regular basis, they must be able to run quickly over a short distance. This is important because they need to be able to catch breakaway shots or beat an opponent to the ball. As such, being able to race to the ball at speed is a must have ability. The best way to develop your sprint-power is through sprinting challenges or through interval training. For sprinting challenges, what you do is continually try to beat your best time. Just have someone with a stopwatch standing by who can monitor your progress over a set distance. Also ask them to encourage you as you race against the clock. You'll be surprised at how a bit of spurring from the side can improve your performance. Interval training is another effective and simple approach. It involves alternating between low and high-intensity activities.

2. *Accuracy is a necessary asset*: Although many people think of accuracy as something that can only be developed through soccer skills practice, there are actually exercises that can help improve accuracy as well. You can work on the muscular strength of your legs using weights, and various other exercises will target specific muscle groups. For abdominal strength, you can do sit-ups and various callisthenic exercises. Although abdominal strength does not seem like a necessary asset, your core is very important in helping to move your entire body with control and precision, therefore helping you to better control most movements with more accuracy.

3. *Strength; the third component*: Want to send that ball flying down the field faster than a speeding bullet? For this you will need good strength, the third component of a sweeper's fitness. As with accuracy, you can develop strength through simple weight exercises as directed by your coach.

4. *Energy reserve & stamina:* Sweepers do not have to move over the length of the field but they are still moving around, and are on high alert for much of the game. This requires a large energy reserve and good stamina. There are many ways to work on stamina, but the most simple is to extend the length of time you are active during practice, and perhaps include a brisk run before and after the session. Again, a coach or trainer is the best person to guide you in this area as they know more about you than anyone else. They will be familiar with your current health and fitness levels, and know what areas you need to improve on the most, and by how much.

5. *Reaction time and reflexes:* Nowhere in the game of soccer are reflexes quite as important as they are in the position of sweeper. Many people think that reaction time is a gift that some are born with more so than others. This might be the case, but it is still a component of fitness nonetheless, and that means it can be developed just like any other skill with the right training. Many players who struggle with reaction time find that simple one-on-one or two-on-one drills helps them to develop the ability to better understand movement, assess it, and then react appropriately.

Physical fitness is crucial to your success as a soccer player whatever your position, but it's particularly important for the position of sweeper. Get to work and push yourself hard in this vital area and your performance on the field will skyrocket.

A lot of soccer players see immediate improvements in the quality of their game when they begin to allocate a portion of their regular practice time for improving fitness levels.

If you are ready to take your game to the next level, then becoming a leaner, meaner super-fit player may well be your best approach.

Opponent's next move

As a sweeper, you will often need to predict your opponent's next move and identify what tactic they are planning to execute.

If you can learn to do this well you will be able to plan your own moves accordingly and take more decisive action as a consequence.

Taking the right actions will result in you turning the game around by sending the ball back to your own offense. It's a simple theory, yet something which is obviously easier said than done.

We're now going to take a look at how a player can learn to read his opponents and predict their future actions.

Many claim that this is a matter of intuition or even extrasensory perception or ESP (the sixth sense), but it is actually a skill that can be learned like all other skills once you know how to go about it.

Below are a few great ways on how to develop this important ability so that you can apply it to your own game:

- *Keep your look low.* A sweeper needs to be following the ball with his eyes, constantly. You may be thinking that this will make things awkward because looking at the ball means you can't be watching the opponent very closely. Well, don't worry, you can do both. This is because you can read what's going on at the ground level; the place where the ball spends most of its time. You see, most opponents give away their intentions by their feet. From the feet, you can see things like where they intend to pass the ball next. This can be read by the position of their supporting foot because the direction of the supporting foot is the same direction of their next pass or kick. While it is easy to fake moves with the eyes or with the body, by using various body feints, it's not so easy for a soccer player to convincingly fake his intentions from the feet. Learn how to read the feet and you'll know what your opponents plan to do next, and without losing your focus on the ball.
- *Judge the importance of movement by its direction.* During a game, soccer players will move up and down the field and also horizontally and diagonally across it. Whenever you see diagonal movement make sure you're on your toes. This usually means that the opposing team is positioning itself for a play of some kind; a play that you now know is about to happen.

- *Pay attention to key players, but...*: Most teams have one or two very talented players on their side. These guys are obviously the ones who dominate much of the action. You can bet that they will be the center of the team's key plays, so watch them carefully and be prepared for any surprises. However, there is a need for some caution here, and that is to not forget about the other guys (the lesser players) on the field. If you only focus your attention on the star players, then it may get picked up by the opposing side. This will mean they have an ideal opportunity to exploit the weakness. Keeping a tight focus only on the key players is a mistake that is made in soccer all the time. In almost every game, an unexpected play is made by someone who was, up until that moment, underestimated. Never underestimate anyone on a soccer field!
- *Watch and learn from your own offense:* Watching your team's offense practice at training sessions can give you an invaluable insight into the way different offensive combinations work, and all from a stress-free perspective. You can then take this knowledge of offensive strategy to your own game. There is only a small list of offensive tactics in the game of soccer, so getting to grips with these will not be hard but they will prove very beneficial.

- *Practice intuition*: You can develop your intuitive perception in a number of ways like playing a game, during practice, or while watching soccer on the television. The idea is to try and predict what certain players are going to do next, and then evaluate your predictions after and learn from them. When you become good at this skill, and you will get good at it providing you practice a lot, you then need to take things to the next stage. This is done by thinking how you would personally respond in the same or similar situation, before, during and after. Don't forget too, that predicting a move is only half of the skill. The other half is what you intend to do next, once your prediction has materialized. This is a thought-and-action process and once you get it, you can then begin to develop your intuition to great effect on the field. Keep in mind that good intuition sometimes derives from nonverbal cues that you don't even notice on a conscious level. In other words, certain intuitions come from what we commonly call "a gut feeling."

Learning how to predict offensive tactics can give you an incredible advantage when playing in the position of sweeper.

Knowing how to watch your opponents and interpret their next moves not only gives you a window into their minds, but it also allows you a bit of time to consider different responses and choose the best option available.

Nowhere in the game of soccer is intuition needed more than in the position of sweeper, and nowhere else will this skill yield such quick and game-changing results.

To Dribble or not to dribble

If you are playing in the position of sweeper, then you may be wondering whether you need to practice your dribbling skills or concentrate more on developing your game in other areas.

This confusion is not uncommon, and what you do depends on a number of factors, including things like the level of your current skills, your competition level, your overall strategy as a sweeper, and of course your coach's opinion.

Some people think that the sweeper's only job is to back up the keeper by defending his goal. This camp believes he should not stray from that arrangement.

In this case, the skill of dribbling is not what you might call essential to his role, but not everyone thinks the sweeper should restrict him to the goal area.

Others believe that a well-rounded sweeper is an asset to the team as he can easily adapt his style of play to suite a given situation. This camp thinks that a sweeper who only protects the defensive third is a waste of a good talent.

Below are a few things worthy of consideration when defining the sweeper role on your team.

- *A sweeper generally should not be in possession of a ball.* To be more precise, the sweeper's role is to take the ball from the opponent and pass it on immediately to another teammate. If played correctly, there shouldn't be an opportunity to possess the ball for more than a few seconds, much less dribble it.
- *A sweeper's job is to sweep.* He is not just another player, but the last man on defense. When the ball is in the sweeper's area, his team is in dire straits because the opponents are now active around the goalmouth; just a hair's breadth away from attempting a shot at the net. This is certainly no time to dribble. Most soccer experts would agree that the sweeper's first action should be to move the ball as far away from the goal area as possible, and in the quickest time conceivable. Such a feat is usually accomplished by a swift hard kick.
- *In many formations, sweepers play a big role in coordinating the defense.* This is because they are often unmarked and can therefore move up and down the field following the ball. This allows them to analyze different situations without too much hassle from the rival side. Sweepers need to be fast-thinking and quick on their feet. If they have possession of the ball on a regular basis, then they will soon find themselves being marked by an opponent. They will then have to focus on protecting the ball, something which is not in the sweeper's job description.

There will always be the occasional situation when dribbling is necessary for the sweeper, for example, when he needs to move the ball to the opposite side of the field before a safe and effective pass can be made. But in general, a sweeper who sticks to his primary role will not be seen dribbling very often.

While every soccer player should know how to dribble on at least a rudimentary level, and that includes the goalie, the sweeper needs to focus the majority of his practice time and energy developing skills which are more specific to his role, skills like shooting, passing, and blocking the goal.

Because the sweeper is responsible for finding and closing holes in the defense, his job is just too important for him to be seen on different parts of the field dribbling and getting involved in other areas of play.

When to speak up

One of the most essential skills for being a good sweeper is effective leadership. This is not something that can be achieved through body language alone.

Whether you are supporting the defense or playing solo, it is imperative that your team understands what you are doing at any given time, and why you are doing it.

They will only be able to back you when you speak up and let them know what your specific intentions are.

The first step to good leadership on the field is clear and effective communication. Obviously you can't spend the entire game in silence, and then expect others to know what you require of them.

Knowing when and how to communicate effectively is fundamental for any sweeper if he's to be effective in delegating tasks to the players around him.

Below are a few situations when a sweeper should make sure he is heard loud and clear.

1. *When a play isn't working*: Because the sweeper has a unique vantage point from where he can view the game, he may be the first to see when a play isn't working. Sharing his observations with the team can prevent them from wasting any more valuable time on a failing strategy by then moving promptly on with another approach.

2. *When there are holes in the defense*: Sometimes a part of the game may not be working out very well, thus allowing the opposing team to exploit the weakness and wreak havoc. A sweeper can recognize when the team isn't taking care of business, and then quickly assign someone to plug any of the gaps he might identify.

3. *When the defensive players need to be reorganized*: There will be times when a particular arrangement simply isn't working. A sweeper is often the first to see this, and as sweeper, he can then move players around to a formation that better suits the needs of the particular situation.

4. *When a teammate needs support*: Not only can the sweeper put out a call for support, but he can also step in himself when a situation warrants it. A sweeper can provide temporary cover for a teammate executing an important play, or help another teammate mark a particularly tricky opponent. This creates a good atmosphere of cooperation within the team.

5. *When the goalie needs to communicate*: Because the goalie is limited to a much smaller area, the sweeper may be called upon to execute a play at the keeper's request, or to communicate the goalie's wishes to the rest of the team.

6. *When the ball is coming toward the goal*: Because a sweeper has the best view of the field, he can often see when the opposing team is making a tactical advance before the other players can. This allows him to act as "town crier," notifying the team that they are under attack.

7. *When the ball is moving forward*. A sweeper is the player who's responsible for clearing the ball away from his goal area. This is the time he needs to speak up and let his centers and forwards know that an opportunity is coming their way.

Not only is a sweeper free to observe the field and the game from a great vantage point, but he's also free to speak up when it's time to better organize the other players.

Using his freedom wisely to help the team achieve victory can make the sweeper a de facto team leader. If he does a good job consistently, then he will become the star player that the team needs and respects.

Building intuition

If you are looking for a soccer position that requires a combination of physical talent and intellectual gifts, then the sweeper is the most obvious choice for you.

As the last line of defense between opponents and the goal, the sweeper needs the freedom to assess and respond to situations whenever and wherever they may arise on the field.

However, this freedom can, at times, be a detriment as well as an advantage. The reason it can be a disadvantage is because it's all too easy to become distracted or to end up far away from the demands of your own goal area.

This can and does happen with less talented or less experienced sweepers. This is why a sweeper needs to have good intuition and know where he should be and when he should be there at any given time.

This position, more than any other in the game of soccer, requires a natural instinct that tells him precisely what his imminent duties are.

Good instinct is perhaps the most important sweeper skill of all. It means having the ability to intuitively know how to handle a situation, often with split second timing.

Whether you follow nursery school soccer games or world class professionals, you will notice that the best players in the position of sweeper have a real ability to predict the game as it materializes.

A talented and experienced sweeper will see plays develop long before anyone else does, and he always seems to know exactly where he should position himself for maximum benefit.

A good sweeper can see the big picture on the field and avoid getting caught up in the minor details.

A surprising number of soccer players shy away from the position of sweeper because they don't think they have what is required to do the job effectively, especially in regards to the intuition aspect.

To be honest, it does take a lot, and it's not a position that suits everyone. Having said that, even though some guys seem to have natural intuition, that doesn't mean it's something you either have or you don't.

Improving intuition is a skill, and although it is more natural in some people than it is in others, it is still a skill, and that means it can be developed just like any other skill can.

Below are some great suggestions on how to develop intuitiveness. Follow these closely and you too could become a serious candidate for the sweeper position on your team.

- *Keep your eyes on the prize*: A good sweeper cannot predict what is happening next if he doesn't know what is happening right now. He mustn't let anything distract him from following the ball and the key players on the opposing team.

- *Scan the field regularly*: Although it is important to watch the ball, the sweeper should also take note of what other key plays are happening elsewhere on the field. These can give clues as to what will probably happen next, thus allowing him to position himself accordingly. Players who are considered to possess good intuition are quite often just guys with a high attention span and an ability to notice details that matter.
- *Stay near the goal box*: The sweeper should avoid moving toward the midfield or the flanks of the field, expect on those occasions when there appears to be little alternative. Not only is the goal box the most obvious place to defend the goal, but it is also the best vantage point for a sweeper. From the center, he can see all the action on the field in one sweeping glance. This unique position makes it much harder for opponents to sneak up and surprise him. An effective sweeper needs to be able to see the whole field more often than not, and that means staying near the goal box.
- *Follow your instincts or gut*: The only way to develop your intuition so that you can become a more instinctive player is through trial and error. Making mistakes, and then learning from them, is an essential step toward becoming a confident and discerning sweeper.

- *Don't play other positions:* Because sweepers are free to move around the field, they sometimes end up taking over their teammates' duties. While even pros sometimes fall into this trap, it's important to avoid it at all costs. Don't become just another defensive player. Make what you do habitual so that it becomes more difficult to stray.
- *Have someone videotape your games and practices:* Quite often, factors that aren't overly obvious during a competition or practice session can actually be much easier to identify when reviewed on recorded media. This "reviewing" is best done at a time when adrenaline has gone and things are generally much calmer. By reviewing your game objectively you will be able to see the cause and effect relationships and learn what cues to watch for in future.

Sweepers with superior intuition have a winning combination of both natural ability and years of practice. Although instinct can be a little difficult to learn, it is by no means impossible.

You can begin to develop this important skill by practicing hard and trying to incorporate the above suggestions into your own style of play.

Fullback's (FB/RB/LB) – Real Life Soccer Heroes

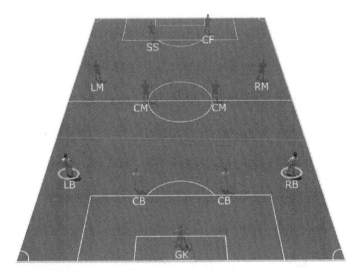

Fullbacks are the super heroes of their soccer team. They wait patiently in the wings of the field until the time is right, and then swoop in to save the day.

Don't think their position on the sides make them any less important than other players because that's just not the case.

Aside from their patience, fullbacks are often among the strongest players on a team, displaying strengths in all three areas, namely technical, physical and mental.

If you want to be a fullback, you should know by the end of this section whether you have what it takes to fulfill this exciting and challenging role.

The role of a fullback

Though positioned on the flanks, the fullback is always in the center of the action. The fullback is located right there in the middle of the center line, dutifully defending his side of the field.

Fullbacks have a dual role which is both offensive and defensive. They must take possession of the ball and then take it down along the outside lines to the offensive third, where it can then be passed on to the team's forwards.

Although this sounds simple in theory, it is, like all positions on a soccer field, a lot easier said than it is to accomplish.

Benefits and drawbacks

An obvious benefit to being a fullback is that it's a position which sees a lot of action. As fullback, you will always be right there in the thick of the action, doing your bit to determine the fate of the game.

Another benefit to being a fullback is that you will be constantly on the move, therefore making this the ideal position for anyone who hates being confined to a small area.

However, the fullback's job is not all strawberries and cream as there are drawbacks to this position too.

One drawback that puts a lot of players off is that a fullback rarely has the opportunity to score goals, or any other glamorous opportunities to impress with.

Even when he is on the offensive, he is still more than likely to end his play by passing the ball to an offensive player so that they can score.

As you can see, this is a position for a solid player, someone who puts the team first and foremost, above his own glory.

It is definitely not a position for an attention-hog, the type who looks for opportunities to shine above the pack.

Another drawback to being a fullback is that it can sometimes be difficult to maintain position in relationship to the ball.

There will be occasions when a fullback wants to move backwards, into the defensive third. Before doing this, he must always make sure the ball is in front of him.

Staying in formation is a key challenge, but committed players soon get used to it, even though it's a hassle at times.

Necessary skills

As a key player, a fullback must possess a long list of skills that are crucial to his success. If you want to be a fullback, then you will need to acquire and maintain excellent technique in areas such as crossing, heading, and tackling.

Accuracy and precision, combined with good overall strength, help to make a fullback's passes impressive and accurate.

Intuition is a good trait for fullbacks to have too, especially if they are strong in other areas where they can also be of use.

Many of the most successful fullbacks have an uncanny ability to take possession of the ball in situations where it seemed practically impossible.

This is something which is accomplished by a combination of their intuition (which allows them to predict the movements of an opponent) and their superior technical skills.

Necessary personality traits

Patience is an important characteristic of any successful fullback. Being able to wait patiently for an opponent to slip up, instead of tackling him head on, can result in winning the ball without any referee interference.

This 'patient approach' can therefore reduce the need to tackle in a sport where a tiny slip up in a tackling attempt can, and quite often does, result in a yellow or red card.

Another important trait for this position is courage. A fullback will often find himself in one-on-one incidents where controlled aggression and true grit can become the decisive factor in determining the outcome of a particular situation.

Finally, a fullback needs to display initiative. The opposing team will be pulling out all the stops to score a goal and the fullback should be putting the same effort into stopping them from succeeding.

With good initiative, a talented fullback will be able to maintain the upper hand in fast moving situations, times where decisive action is essential to a successful outcome.

If you decide to take on this position, just know that it doesn't matter whether you play as a left or right fullback, you will still have a challenging job ahead of you, with responsibilities in both defense and offense.

There is nothing quite as rewarding as a demanding job that's done well. The fullback position is certainly a challenging job and one that is incredibly rewarding when performed with skill and commitment.

Beating fast running forwards

Fullbacks play a crucial role in the game of soccer. Like all center and defensive players, their objective is to keep the opposing team from scoring goals.

Fullbacks also protect teammates who are moving in to score. It is imperative that they are alert, proactive, and extremely fast.

Anyone who plays the position of left or right fullback is truly indispensable to their team.

Speed is of the essence for the role of fullback. This is no job for an average runner. Even those with good speed and stamina can still find it difficult at times as they try to keep up with the often insane pace that the position demands.

Not only do they have to beat the fast running forwards of the opposing team, but they must also stay wide and provide overlapping coverage on the field.

This means that fullbacks are covering a lot of area, and the only way to do that successfully is to have the ability to run with at an incredible pace.

If you are, or think you could be, a gifted fullback, yet lack somewhat in the speed department, then here are a few ways to help you beat those fast running forwards:

- *Warmup and cool down properly*: Nothing will slow you down as quickly as tired or injured muscles. This is something which is bound to occur if your body isn't treated with the respect that it deserves. Make sure you take the time to stretch and warm up your muscles before playing or practice. After all, your muscles take enough of a beating as it is when playing soccer. So any failure to warmup and cool down before and after games or practice is only going to hinder, not help, your development.
- *Pace yourself*: While there is a lot of ground to cover, do so in a natural stride unless the situation demands more of you. This will leave you with enough energy to sprint when approaching the opposing team's speedy forwards.
- *Practice distance running and speed*. Both of these running strategies are absolutely essential to the positions of left and right fullback. Distance running will train you to pace yourself and maintain good stamina throughout the game, while sprinting trains the body to respond quickly in fast moving situation.

- *When possible, use the laws of physics.* Every fourth grader knows that the shortest distance between two points is in a straight line, so don't waste time and energy by needlessly zigzagging around the field when it's not necessary. Similarly, don't attempt to dribble the ball if you can get it to the same destination by passing it to a teammate. With so much physical activity required of your position, there really is no need to add further to the pain.
- *Defend deep*: This means stay in the defensive third of the field and meet the forwards on the battlefield. This is a much better approach than following them from one side of the field to the other. Not only will this tactic conserve your energy, but it will reduce the number of goals made from breakaway runs.

The golden rule you most need to remember, whether playing as a left or right fullback, is to work smart and avoid working unnecessarily hard.

There are enough stresses on this physically demanding position already, without adding any needless work to it by overexerting yourself and following wrong strategies.

Push your body close to its limits when a situation requires that of you, but if you start trying to push yourself beyond your limits, then you're on a hiding to nothing.

If you want a great example of how too much unnecessary effort, along with the wrong strategy, can result in total failure, then have a read of that classic children's story, " The Tortoise and the Hare." It sums everything up perfectly.

Following up in the offense

The fullback position is one of the most versatile in the game of soccer. It is unique because fullbacks get to play both a defensive and an offensive game.

However, a lot of fullbacks tend to neglect their offensive role and remain on defensive duty at all times. This results in the offense cleaning up after them.

As a fullback, one of your key duties is to mark opponents, as well as to use tackling and other techniques to take possession of the ball.

Most fullbacks excel in this area and are experts at taking the ball effectively and legally. It's what they do next, or more specifically, don't do next, where many fall short.

The main reason why so many fullbacks are reluctant to follow through once they get possession of the ball, is because they worry that they don't have the speed or the stamina necessary to successfully take it down the field. But how can this be so?

Anyone who has seen a fullback in action knows that they have plenty of speed, skill, and stamina that they could use to run with the ball after winning a duel.

In fact, fullbacks are among the strongest players on a soccer team, and they have the physical abilities to move the ball down five soccer fields if they had to.

All it takes is a little self-confidence and some initiative. So their problem is more likely due to a lack of self-confidence than a physical inability.

Another reason why fullbacks stay in the defense is that they don't want to face down the opposing team's defense.

This is something that can be an intimidating experience, especially for a green fullback or a defensive player who is used to being the tackler and not the one being tackled.

However, just like any other fear, the only way to really deal with a thing is to face it. Whenever a fear is challenged head-on a few times, then the problem soon becomes a thing of the past.

As a fullback you will need to get used to facing opponents, so simply apply your assertiveness without giving to much thought to the situation.

Do this and your fears and apprehensions will quickly disappear, and that in turn will free you up to concentrate on more important things, like performing at you best without being hindered by fears and self-doubts.

There are some fullbacks who worry that they don't have the offensive skills necessary to take the ball all the way.

This is probably because they mostly train as defensive players, and so that's where their main focus lies. But even this excuse is made into a bigger issue than it actually is.

You see, most defensive skills, such as dribbling and passing, translate well on the offensive field as well.

Granted, there are some skills which are unique to offensive play, but these can be quickly learned through drills and regular practice, and then bolted on to the fullbacks existing arsenal of abilities.

However, many amateur fullbacks like to get rid of the ball as quickly as possible, even though this is not usually the best strategy.

There are more good reasons to follow up in the offense with a retaken ball than there are to pass it on.

The most experienced players get a lot of satisfaction in following up the ball themselves. These guys wouldn't dream of passing it on like a hot coal, just so that someone else can finish the job.

Another reason why passing the ball on is a bad choice is because there's always the risk that it will be intercepted by a member of the opposing team, not least because the center of the field tends to be more crowded with players than the flanks.

It is usually better and safer for the fullback to move the ball to the offensive third by himself.

And finally, fullbacks who attempt to follow up in the offense are in a good position to succeed. This is because the other team will most probably not expect this to happen, and so they get caught off guard.

Sometimes a fullback can take the ball all the way to the offensive third completely uncontested.

The reason he can do this is because the opponents fail to see him coming.

These are the plays that legends are made of, and they are great morale boosters and talking points for years to come. He who dares wins!

So although the fullback is traditionally a defensive position, it is also one with a strong offensive component to it.

As a fullback, you can maximize your abilities by using them for both the defense and the offense.

No other position allows so much versatility as the fullback. So why not seize the opportunity to shine and take the ball all the way down the field and transform that tackle of yours into a goal.

Don't run with the ball for too long

Fullbacks have plenty of things to occupy their time. They lurk on the flanks, waiting for an opportunity to step in and take the ball, and once they have it, you'd better watch out!

A really experienced fullback has the speed and ball-handling skills to take the ball all the way down the field to the offensive third and sometimes even all the way to the goal.

There are some fullbacks who are quite the opposite of the reluctant types we looked at earlier. These players can go too far with their confidence though, and become just a bit too eager too often.

One of the most common traps of a right or left fullback is transporting the ball for too long when another move would have proven more effective.

Let us take a look at the "too long," concept and put it into some perspective. The main objective of a soccer game is to simply score goals and prevent the other side from doing the same.

If you are running out of energy and starting to lose focus before you've completed your run, then you are probably transporting the ball for too long.

If you are transporting the ball for a good distance when you could have passed it to a teammate to achieve the same outcome (obviously with less effort), then you are not only transporting the ball for too long, but you're also depleting your valuable energy stores in the process. In cases like these you are working unnecessarily hard.

If you also find that your team is not finishing their offensive plays with viable shots, then you may also be transporting the ball too long.

If any of these situations are plaguing your team, then it's time to find other options.

Luckily, there are ways to avoid this common trap. Below are some simple, alternative strategies that can be a lot more energy efficient and produce more favorable outcomes than transporting the ball too long:

- *Pass to an offensive player.* Look around for an open forward and pass the ball to them. This will move the ball faster and with less chance of interception. You will also use less energy.
- *Cross the ball to a midfielder.* A midfielder may have a straight shot at one of the forwards and be able to pass the ball on to them. If so, then use him.

- *If you are close enough, shoot.* Although shooting is not one of your primary duties, opportunities will definitely come up from time to time. Many fullbacks decide, unwisely, to give up these opportunities and transport the ball over to a forward instead. Never, ever, pass on a chance to shoot. You never know when you will score a surprise goal, and you'll be all the more popular for it.

Another very good reason why you shouldn't transport the ball too far for too long is that you need to stay in the proximity of your position.

If you stray too far then you can't be of maximum benefit to the team.

Your coach has planned your formation for a reason, and you disrupt that arrangement every time you stray.

Whenever a fullback transports the ball for some distance he becomes distracting by upsetting the team formation.

There is always plenty for a fullback to do with his main duties so it's better to adhere to the role. Unless situations warrant it, the fullback should really leave the risky maneuvers to the forwards.

Lastly, as a fullback you must conserve your energy so that you can perform well in your position as required.

There will be plenty of running around for you to do as it is, without burning yourself out with unnecessary maneuvers.

Remember, your objective is to play smart, and that means you should conserver your energy for when you really need it most.

There will be occasions when transporting the ball is absolutely the right choice. The thing to do is always weigh up the options first.

Make it a hard and fast rule to use another simpler, safer, more energy-efficient approach whenever it makes better sense.

Your team depends on you to be the very best fullback you can be; using your better judgment is part of this.

First and foremost, your job is to take the ball to the offensive third of the field and deliver it to your forwards.

How you do this is not as important as how quickly and how effectively you can achieve it.

Fullbacks and the offside rule

There are very few drawbacks to being a fullback in the game of soccer. This position basically has a limitless reign of the field, with a strong role in both defense and offense.

Fullbacks wait in the flanks, ready to step in and assist at a moment's notice.

They can literally pop up from nowhere at times, taking control of situations that can make all the difference to the outcome of a game.

Perhaps the biggest negative of this position is that fullbacks are notorious for breaking the very complicated offside rule, and frequently.

This can be become a real disadvantage to both the player and his team if he doesn't' get to grips with offside rule.

This is something which is easier said than done for some players, especially in high-tempo games. The offside rule can be confusing for fullbacks as they play both offensive and defensive roles on the team.

The offside rule basically states that any player on the opposing half of the field who is closer to the opposition goal than the ball and the last defender, is then in the offside position.

Although this might at first sound like a confusing rule to those new to the game of soccer, it is not as complex as it seems, nor is it difficult to maintain the correct position on the field.

In fact, it's quite easy to stay on your side providing you keep a few simple rules in mind. Below are the situations in which you are never offside:

- When you are behind or next to the soccer ball (closer to your goal).
- When you are on your own half of the soccer field (the side your goal is on).
- When you receive the ball from a corner kick, goal kick, or throw in.
- When you pass the ball backward.
- When you personally have possession of the ball, making you the first non-goalie defender.

This is a far flung and varied set of circumstances but it pays to remember them all.

If you are found offside when playing in the position of fullback, then the other team is likely to be awarded an indirect free kick, which is basically a free road straight to your goal.

Below are two other common situations where your opponents might be awarded a free kick when you break the offside rule:

- You are in an offside position, other than any of the above five situations, as the ball is being played by one of your own teammates.
- You or your team gains an advantage by you being in an offside position. Examples might include your offside position interferes with your opponent's plays or you are distracting the opposing goalkeeper.

You really have to be especially careful when passing the ball to teammates.

Even if you are not offside when in possession of the ball, if you pass the ball to a teammate who is closer to your side of the field than you are, then you may be declared offside.

Because there are so many rules here, there is often a lot of interpretation that's left up to judges.

For this reason, it is always a good idea to stay as clearly "onside" as you can, especially while you team is making crucial plays.

If there is anything worse than having a play interrupted by an official, it's having that official award the opposing team a free kick.

Always stay several steps behind the ball and you will never be in violation of the offside rule, and therefore never lose out to this common fullback mistake.

As you can see, the offside rule has many facets, but it is worth your time getting to fully understand this rule along with all of its variations and applications to the different circumstances.

Take the time to understand what it means to be onside, and avoid being just another fullback who broke the rules and gave their opponents an advantage.

It's hard enough trying to win a game against a talented opposition as it is, without giving them a helping hand.

Clearing the ball

As you now know, the fullback spends a lot of his time in both an offensive and a defensive role. However, no single duty is quite as important as clearing the ball away.

Knowing how to use this essential skill, and the times where it's most appropriate to utilize it, can make all the difference to the quality of your game.

OK, let us now look at what it means exactly to "clear the ball."

Firstly, clearing the ball is something which is crucial for those occasions when the ball is within scoring range of your goal.

This is a time where there's a real risk of the opponents attempting a swift shot at your goal. Whenever the ball is successfully cleared away in these situations, everyone gets to breathe easy again.

Clearing the ball is obviously a defensive measure that can, when employed correctly, make scoring practically impossible for the opposing team.

If you are a fullback and have mastered how to successful clear the ball in tricky situations, then you will undoubtedly become one of the star players in your team.

The rule of thumb is that you should always clear the ball whenever it ends up within scoring range of your goal.

Just how you clear the ball is not as important as actually doing it, but obviously you will need some sharp skills in order to be successful at this, namely dribbling, passing, crossing, and ball handling.

While these foundational skills are important, it's also essential that you know how to follow through with your actions, particularly in situations where there's an opportunity to do something useful with the ball after clearing it.

You will need to know who you intend to pass the ball to, or what to do in an event where all traditional options are closed to you. In other words, you have to be one step ahead of the game.

Avoid locking your focus on just the task at hand by having a firm idea of what you intend to do after your immediate actions.

Fullbacks can often clear the ball most effectively by kicking it directly to their own team's fullbacks and midfielders.

Along with teaching clearing skills to defenders, it's also important to teach fullbacks and midfielders the importance of staying within a reasonable passing range of the defensive players whenever the ball is on the defensive third of the field.

From here, they must fight for the ball with the same initiative and assertiveness that the fullback used to clear it and pass it over to their domain.

Sometimes there will be no obvious person to clear the ball to.

In situations like these it is important for fullbacks to use discretion and come up with a "plan B" before their attack.

If there is no imminent danger of the opposing team retaking possession of the ball, then the fullback has options.

He might try dribbling the ball to a safer position, as one example, or take it further up the field to the offensive end. Or maybe there are other plays that look like reasonable options at the time.

In situations when there is no player ready to receive the ball, nor are there any other smart choices available because the opposing team is moving in too fast, then the fullback may have to resort to extreme measures such as kicking the ball over the end line, resulting in a corner kick, or kicking it over the side line, which will result in a throw in.

Though not ideal, these extreme measures are still better options than allowing the opposing team to regain possession of the ball so close to your goal.

It's also important to be fearless in your decision making.

So make sure you're never afraid to be nontraditional or even a little cheeky when it comes to protecting your goal.

Even extreme measures are better than watching an opponent score while your team stands idly by, powerless to do anything about it.

Fullbacks who are still learning the role should practice their "last resort" moves along with the midfielders and forwards who will be backing them up.

Midfielders should practice receiving the ball and taking it forward to the offensive end. The fullbacks, for their part, should learn how to quickly and effectively clear the ball over to the midfielders.

If your team uses a "shift and sag" formation, they should have no trouble maintaining coverage while moving the ball away from the danger zone.

Clearing the ball is a simple yet essential skill. It's a move which can help fullbacks change the course of the game whenever they are able to clear the ball away from the "danger zone" and move it swiftly on to their teammates.

Mastering this area of defense will result in fewer goals made against you, and more scoring opportunities for your side because you. In other words, it's winning combination.

Don't let another goal make it by you when it can be stopped with a simple plan of action.

Wingback (WB/RWB/LWB) - A Super Dynamo

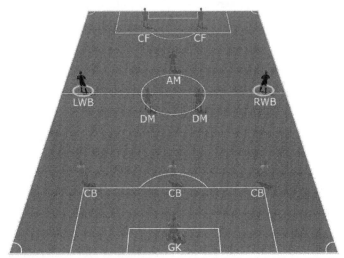

Ever thought about playing in the position of left or right wingback? Wingbacks might not have real wings, but they can often be seen flying into action as they swoop into difficult situations and save the day.

Having a well-trained and well-disciplined wingback can make the difference between winning and losing games. If you have the speed of an eagle and the eyes of a hawk, then playing as either the left or right wingback might turn out to be the perfect position for you.

What is a wingback?

As the name suggests, the position of wingback is a cross between winger and fullback. In general, a wingback is a soccer player who plays the fullback position, but on the far left or far right of the field.

As with the fullback position, the wingback has both offensive and defensive duties and is therefore required to possess a diverse range of basic and specialized skills.

Wingers need to excel in a variety of situations.

They need aggressiveness so that they can fearlessly take possession of the ball when the situation warrants it, plus they need stamina and good overall soccer skills to deliver the ball all the way to the forwards.

Despite these abilities, wingbacks are primarily midfielders and must have the solid skills required of this position as well.

Essential skills

A wingback is often the most athletically gifted player on the team. In fact, when you think of the best players on most teams, amateur and professional, it is often the wingbacks that spring to mind more often than not.

These athletes must run up and down the field tirelessly and have plenty of energy to spare when other players are flagging. Stamina is a must-have quality for this position.

Without stamina you would find yourself breathless after just a few minutes of the starting whistle, and that would result in you becoming a burden to the side.

The ability to recover quickly is not an option. Wingbacks need to change gears as often as the soccer ball changes players.

As a wingback, you will need to possess good basic skills such as dribbling, passing, and tackling.

Essential personality traits

There are certain personality traits that definitely help an individual to become a better wingback.

Courage is a must-have personal characteristic. This is because wingbacks often have to go up against the other team's best and most aggressive players, and that's not a job for the faint-hearted.

Intuition is another trait that makes the job of wingback so much easier.

This is because intuition allows a player to better predict what the other team is planning, or potentially planning to do next.

He can then go on to make better informed decisions based on his intuition.

Benefits and drawbacks

One of the benefits of being a wingback is that you are physically and strategically at the center of the game. Very few important plays go down without at least some involvement from the team's wingbacks.

Another benefit of the wingback position is that it requires a variety of skills due to the high amount of activity and situations the player faces.

This makes it a great job for anyone who gets easily bored by a lack of action, as is the case in some other positions, or by limited opportunities to practice all the skills he has trained so hard to master.

The major drawback of playing in the wingback position is that it offers very little in the way of glory.

Although wingbacks are involved in many parts of the game, their role is still largely one of support.

Whether they are supporting the strikers or backing up the defense, there is little opportunity for a wingback to shine.

Should you play as a wingback?

Before you decide whether the wingback position is the right one for you or not, it's always a good idea to start asking yourself a few basic questions.

You answers to these questions will undoubtedly help you to make much better informed decisions.

The first and most fundamental question you need to ask yourself is whether you have the basic skills required to play the part, or at have least the initiative and willpower to develop them.

Another essential question is that of stamina. Do you have the stamina required to maintain the high energy levels needed for the entire duration of a game?

What about the lack of glory the role comes with? Despite your best efforts on the field, you will rarely be the player who stands out above the others.

Are you really willing to take a back seat from the spotlight and let others take most of the glory, often as result of you assisting in their success?

Despite lacking in glamour, the wingback position is definitely not a thankless one.

If nurturing ego is not your thing, and you are far more interested in the opportunity to make a difference to the team as a whole, than you are basking in fame, then this is probably the perfect position for you.

Wingbacks need to be solid, strong players from both a physical and mental perspective.

The wingbacks' duties depend on what the team is doing at any given time. When the team is defending, the wingback plays as a defender.

When the team is attacking, the wingback plays as a winger. This multi-tasking means a wingback has to carry the weight of two players.

If you think you have the stamina, initiative, and necessary skills to carry this load, then the only thing left for you to do is to put your name forward as the team's wingback.

Rules about dribbling

The position of wingback is one of the more modern soccer positions. It can be defined as a fullback with extra attacking capabilities.

To be a good wingback requires a very specific and specialized set of skills and abilities.

If you are already a wingback on your team, you have been chosen because you meet a long and particular set of necessary abilities.

However, because this is still a relatively new position in soccer's history, there are a lot of contradictions regarding the actual role and duties of a wingback.

If you're still looking into the possibility of playing as a wingback, then you are probably finding that there are more questions than there are answers on the specifics of the position.

When you should dribble is probably one of those questions where the answer seems pretty cloudy at best.

Although there are no hard and fast rules, below are a few things that you should definitely keep in mind with regards to the dribbling role of a wingback.

- *Soccer players should never dribble when they could pass, unless there is an impending scoring opportunity:* This rule is the same for wingbacks. Dribbling is a high risk activity where there's a lot of potential risk for losing the ball. Passing makes more sense if an opportunity is open.

- *The midfield can become crowded and difficult to navigate during a lively game*: If dribbling can keep you out of this quagmire of players, then it might be a good option, in fact it might be your only option, depending on the situation. If dribbling looks likely to take you into the heart of the teeming masses, then quickly find another way of moving the ball on. Taking a soccer ball into a crowd of hungry players is a surefire way of losing it.
- *Dribbling holds you back*: Every step you take while in possession of the ball is a step that takes you away from your primary function as a wingback, which is attacking the ball and moving it forward. Don't let dribbling take up time that could interfere with your core duties.
- *Do what works.* When all said and done, this is what makes a great soccer player in any position:

Knowing what will save a situation and how to successfully pull it off is the one X-factor that sets star soccer players apart from the rest.

Dribbling is always the right choice if it leads to the best outcome, and it is always the wrong choice when it sets your team back.

Whenever an opportunity presents itself, always move quickly and without reservation.

Ironically, one of the most common criticisms of those who play in the position of wingback is that they have poor dribbling skills.

This should tell you how unimportant dribbling skills are to your position on the team.

At the end of the day, if a good dribbling ability was a necessary skill for wingbacks, then those without it wouldn't get offered the position.

Even so, a wingback still needs to possess some aptitude for dribbling as there will always be occasions where it's the only option.

As a wingback, discretion and intuition will be two of your most vital attributes. Practice often and let your sixth sense, along with these suggestions, be your guide.

Knowing when to dribble is a skill on its own and one that can only be learned in the context of regular practice and real live games.

Wingback, not midfielder

Because wingbacks and midfielders are playing within close proximity of each other, it's easy for them to get their unique roles and duties mixed up. To help clarify the main differences, here are the definitions of the two unique positions.

- A wingback is basically a blend of winger and fullback. While they have the defensive capabilities of a fullback, they have the additional demands of an attacking position.
- Midfielders are players whose range of play is in the center third of the field, between forwards and the defensive players.

As you can see, there is a lot of overlap between the two positions.

While it is easy to see how a wingback might become confused about his game on occasion, it is important to remember to stay within the confines of one's own position. The primary role of a wingback is attacking the ball, first and foremost.

A midfielder's primary role differs to that of a wingback. His job is to take possession of the ball and act as a transition between the two outer thirds of the field.

Wingers should avoid performing this type of task. There are usually more than enough midfielders to adequately perform these duties on their own.

So the wingback should be acting more offensively, albeit outside of the offensive section of the field.

Wingbacks should be backing up the strikers and keeping the ball in their possession until the time is right to pass it on.

There are plenty of center backs and other defensive players around, so wingbacks don't usually need to play a defense role.

The main reason a wingback, or any other position on the field, should avoid performing duties other than those specific to their role, is because it can become confusing for the other team players.

Every player should know exactly what part he has on the team and adhere to the specific duties of his role unless a particular situation dictates otherwise.

Stepping into the role of other positions, no matter how briefly, will result in valuable time being lost as other player's attempt to fathom out what's going on with the ball.

Likewise, when play becomes somewhat ragtag, the opposition then has more opportunity to steal the ball away.

There is a very good reason why the positions on a soccer team are so thoroughly divided.

When the game was first invented, the basic arrangement of the various positions proved to be the most effective way of playing the game.

Whenever a player fails to recognize, or simply decides not to adhere to the specific duties of his position for some reason, then that creates an atmosphere of chaos.

And whenever chaos is present, that makes it almost impossible for the team to function properly as a well-oiled unit.

Furthermore, when a wingback takes over the duties of another position, such as a midfielder, it bogs him and the side down as he attempts to perform well in a role that he hasn't been trained for.

Midfielders, like those in other positions on the field, were specifically chosen for their skills.

These abilities will have been honed in on through hours, weeks, and months of hard work as the players strived to develop the skills needed for their specific position.

By sticking to what you know, to what you do best, therefore, will produce the best possible outcome for you and your team.

You can't possibly be available as a wingback when you're running off to play the part of another position mid-game.

Imagine the scenario where a striker suddenly needs the support of his wingback and there's nobody there.

This can easily happen if you've not yet returned to position after completing some other duty, unrelated to that of a wingback.

No one wants to let their side down by not coming through when they're most needed, especially when that letdown is caused by an unnecessary blunder, like momentarily taking on the role of another position.

It can be tempting wanting to help out another position when you seem to have a spare moment, but be that as it may, you should avoid making this a regular practice.

Instead, stick to what you know, which in this case is to remain as the team's wingback.

Another downside to butting in and performing an action other than what belongs to your winger duties, is that it might go completely wrong.

When this happens, the last thing you will be seen as by your teammates is a hero for having a go. You will probably be scorned as someone who is irresponsible and egotistical.

Avoiding unnecessary rushes

Playing in the position of a wingback can be exhausting.

If you're as actively involved in a competition as you should be, then you ought to be feeling pretty tired by the end of the game, despite being young, fit, and super healthy.

This unique blend of winger and fullback gets a lot of action in most soccer games. It's therefore important that you don't waste your energy unnecessarily.

Despite this advice being repeated countless times by coaches everywhere, wingbacks continue to tire themselves out for no good reason.

The result of their overexertion is that they have very little energy for when they need it the most. When this happens, they become the weakest link in the team.

Ask any experienced soccer coach how wingbacks waste valuable energy, and the number one response will more than likely be by unnecessary rushes.

In the game of soccer, a rush is basically a play in which a wingback, or other defensive player, aggressively pursues a ball that's in the possession of an opponent.

Obviously there are times when a rush is justified, and therefore necessary, but there are plenty of other times when it's totally the wrong move to make. Below are some examples of both cases, starting first with justified rushes.

Rush when:
- An opponent has the opportunity to shoot and score if left to his own devices.
- You are closely matched to your opponent in skill, size, and energy.
- You have a good plan, meaning you know how to effectively retake the ball.
- There is no player better positioned than you to take possession of the ball.

- Rushing is the only option to take control of the ball.

As you can see, taking off after the ball is sometimes a good idea or it's the only sensible option at the time given the circumstances.

OK, let's now look at those times when rushing after the ball is a downright terrible idea for a wingback.

Don't rush when:

- You don't have an offensive back up. A rush at this point will likely be a colossal waste of your energy.
- There is another teammate closer to the situation and more capable of handling it without assistance.
- You are overmatched. When an opponent is bigger, stronger, or simply less worn out than you are, this is a time to pass and let someone better matched take over.
- You have to commit a rule violation to make a successful rush.

As you can see from the examples above, there are times when rushing should definitely be avoided.

If you perform rushes in any of the above situations, then there's a good likelihood that you've got into the bad habit of rushing for the wrong reasons more often than not.

Not only can this approach prove disastrous to your energy levels, but it can also destroy your morale and therefore your ability to play soccer at your best.

While it is important to give 100% of yourself to every game, you still need to pace yourself properly and know how to conserve energy.

You certainly don't want to be burning up any of that finite energy of yours by rushing after the ball in all the wrong situations.

So the key to succeeding in your position as wingback is to be a good steward of your stamina; conserving your precious effort and energy for the times when it is going to pay off for you and your team.

Knowing how to balance the needs of the team, along with the limitations of your body, is one skill that will always set amateurs apart from the professionals.

The importance of crosses

The cross is defined, in its most basic form, the kicking of a ball from one side of the field to the center or to the other side. That's about it.

Good, well-aimed crosses are important because they move the ball from one part of the field to the other quickly, and with minimal risk of interception.

Whenever a winger crosses the ball to a forward or a striker, he's not just moving it on to a different player on another part of the field; he's also creating an opportunity for them to score from that cross.

Indeed, scoring is the primary end purpose of crossing. For that reason, always cross with some idea of how the player receiving the ball will utilize it to best effect.

Crossing is an easy skill to learn on a superficial level, but mastering it fully will require a bit more time and effort.

As a wingback, you should take the ball down the outside of the field without letting it get intercepted by opponents. You then need to locate a teammate who is open to receiving your ball so that you can make your cross. If you are close to the teammate who will receive the ball, simply pass it over and let him work his magic.

If the teammate is some distance away, you may decide to chip the ball over to him.

Note that most crosses are airborne, although this is not a hard and fast rule as it depends on the individual situations.

If the teammate receiving the ball is close to the opponent's goal, then you might want to send him a low cross.

Low crosses can be received quicker and easier than airborne crosses, so a low cross therefore increases the potential for scoring. As with other types of passes, the outcome of a cross can vary widely, depending on the following:

- The distance the ball has to travel.
- The height of the ball in the air.
- The curve and spin on the ball.

There are four major types of crosses, all of which you will need to know how to perform in order to be a successful wingback. They are:

1. The chip cross
2. The low cross
3. The in swinger
4. The out swinger

The chip cross is as simple as it sounds. The ball is kicked from beneath, thus chipping it into the air and over the head of an opponent to the waiting teammate(s). Forwards and strikers can see a chipped ball easier as it travels toward them.

This enables them to quickly position themselves in preparation for receiving it. This type of cross is typically used when all players involved are near the goal line, and when a low ball can be easily intercepted.

The low cross is as easy as it sounds. The ball is simply kicked to the receiving player keeping low to, or actually along the ground the whole time.

Although many view the low cross as a beginner's move, it can be very appropriate and extremely effective over short distances, especially if your opponents aren't expecting it.

The in-swinger and out-swinger crosses both have a curve, but the difference is where the curve leaves them.

With an in-swinger cross, the ball curves toward the goal, while with an out-swinger cross, it swings away from the goal.

These passes can prove invaluable once they are mastered, not least because their subtle change in direction can often catch opposing defenders and their keeper off guard.

The most important things to consider with regards to knowing when or when not to cross are as follows:

-   Who will be receiving the ball?
-   What can your teammate do with the ball once it's in his possession?
-   What are the chances of the cross being intercepted by an opponent?

In general, a high risk move must always have a high potential for scoring, whereas a low risk move requires less calculation.

Learning how to cross and knowing what type of cross to use will make all the difference to the outcome of your crossing attempts.

Midfield Line - Conducting the Game

Some soccer fans compare the midfield line to a battleground. Others compare it to a powerful machine that constantly changes up and down gears as and when it needs to.

Perhaps the most accurate comparison though, is with the conductor of a symphony orchestra.

Like conductors, a midfield line player sets the tempo for the game and directs others so that there is movement and harmony in all the surrounding action. At least that's the theory.

Just like the great masters of classical music, you must be able to organize, direct, and inspire those you are leading to perform with accuracy and grace. This is what makes a truly great midfield line player.

Some people are born with good leadership skills, whereas others must learn them from scratch.

Fortunately, being an effective leader is a skill that can be learned by those willing to put in the effort.

Having said that, just how effective you become depends a lot on your character and your ability to grasp and develop the areas that need improving.

Leadership is not for everyone though, and some players are happy to be foot soldiers and take direction. Leaders, or those learning to lead, obviously take on different roles/positions to those who follow.

Let's now look a little closer at the specific requirements needed for a good midfield line player.

- *Watch the game carefully*: Be constantly aware of any holes that need filling and act accordingly: Your main job is to look out for any weak spots. When you do identify weaknesses you either fill them yourself or direct other players to step in. If the team is playing offensively, the midfield generally plays forward. If you are playing defensively, it's important to immediately transform into a defensive role by marking opponents and attempting to take the ball. You should be watching the game, predicting your opponent's next moves, and working to counteract them before, or just as, they are about to act.

- *Communicate often*: Effective communication is the only way to make your needs known to others. Communication is also important when it comes to encouraging your teammates. Team morale is essential to the outcome of a game, and there's no better way to raise it than to offer regular verbal support and encouragement.
- *Learn from your mistakes*: In order to lead effectively you must know what direction is best for your team. Learning from mistakes is the only way to develop an effective soccer strategy. While it's important not to dwell on slipups, you should use them to identify your team's weaknesses so that you can continue to improve with every game.
- *Dedication*: Set a good example by working hard at each practice session and during every game. You should always be on time and in uniform. Your teammates will not take direction from you if you do not set a good example and show that you are dedicated to the success of the side. Not only will extra practice and solid technical skills show your team that you care, but they will also help you to maintain and develop the multi-tasking ability that is expected from a midfield line player.

- *Avoid negativity*: Avoiding negativity does not only mean steering clear of verbal criticism, but also any negative body language, and that includes facial expressions that convey disapproval. It's important to be patient with other players and never be too quick to judge. Gaining trust and respect is fundamental for good leadership. Both your leadership position and your teammates' confidence are privileges that must be earned and are not things which can be taken for granted. Staying positive is an important component of good leadership.

Not only is a good midfield line player mindful of all of the above leadership attributes, but he must also play a good game as well, thus making this an extremely challenging role.

Knowing how to play the game means understanding when to be a leader and when to fade into the background as just another player on the team. This is fundamental to the position.

If you can become good at leading, effective at teamwork, and maintain superior technical skills, then you are sure to have a long and illustrious tenure in the game of soccer.

Central Midfielder (CM) - The Wise One

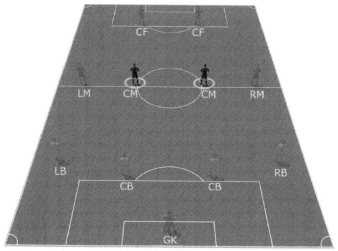

Are you considering the position of central midfielder?

This player is so important to both offensive and defensive sides that he is often referred to as "the playmaker."

There is a very good reason for this nickname. Almost every play in the game will come through this position on the field. That means the ball will be passed to you and from you constantly.

Because this position is crucial to every aspect of game play, it's therefore important to have a well-developed set of skills

Although there is no end to the demands of this position, the list below includes the absolute necessities for succeeding as a central midfielder.

- *Positional awareness*: To be an effective central midfielder you need to be constantly alert, knowing where the ball is, who possesses it, and where you should position yourself next in order to be of maximum benefit to the team. Although you are a midfielder, you should position yourself toward the end of the field where the ball is being played at any given time. If the ball is in your defensive third, you should be marking opponents or pressuring the player with the ball. If your team is on the offensive third, you should be making runs at the ball. Because there are so many facets to this position, the central midfielder player needs to be mindful at all times of his optimal placement in relationship to others.

- *Physical fitness*: Stamina and strength are paramount to a player who will be actively involved in game play at an almost constant level. A central midfielder needs to be able to dribble tirelessly, and that means without becoming easily fatigued or distracted. Although this position doesn't require the bursts of extreme energy that some other positions do, you will, however, be active in the game constantly with little or no downtime.

- *Superior passing skills*: Every player needs passing skills but none quite as much as a central midfielder. A large part of his job boils down to distributing the ball. This means you cannot just be "good" at passing, you have to be the best on your side. You will also need to be a versatile passer, someone who is able to move the ball accurately and swiftly in almost any conceivable situation.
- *Calm under pressure*: Most of the plays a central midfielder is involved in will be executed under extreme pressure from the opposing team. Therefore, you simply cannot allow yourself to be intimidated in stressful situations. If you do become unsettled, then you will lose the focus you need to play quickly and effectively. A successful central midfielder doesn't just perform well in high stress situations, he actually thrives on them.
- *Follow your instincts*: Sometimes quick thinking just isn't quick enough. You need to have foresight so that you can predict what your opponent is likely to do next, and then prepare you next action based on your intuition. Having good instincts will allow you to be proactive instead of reactive.

As you can see from the above, the central midfielder position is one where skill meets strength.

If you think you have the combination of physical and mental talents to play in this position, then there will always be a place for you on the soccer field.

These capable, well rounded individuals can take almost any situation and turn it into a scoring opportunity for their side.

Although central midfielders don't often get the credit they deserve, they truly are the backbone of any good soccer team.

Reading the game

A central midfielder operates in the 'engine room' of the team. He is expected to be active in all areas between the two penalty boxes.

He must contribute to both attack and defense as and when he's needed. A central midfielder has to be a good all-rounder and possess excellent technical and physical attributes.

Most important of all is that a midfielder must be able to read the game, that is, know when to play defensively, how to find space in the middle of the pack, and when to make occasional lung-busting runs into the opposing penalty area.

Examples of great midfielders who can read the game intelligently include the likes of Steven Gerrard, Andrea Pirlo and Xavier "Xavi.

These guys can interpret the game around them so well that they can often predict how play will unfold from moment to moment.

This intuition allows them to get into the right place at the right time, something which is obviously an invaluable asset for the success of any midfielder.

Reading the game well is a mental, rather than a physical or technical skill. It is therefore more difficult to provide an exact set of guidelines on how to develop this aspect of your game.

Increasing "game intelligence" requires experience in game situations, as well as lots of tactical expertise. This expertise includes knowing about your opponent's (and your own) strengths, and more importantly, weaknesses.

Once you have an understanding on this, you are then in a much better position to make better informed decisions.

Below are a few basic pointers that you can follow. These will help you to lay a good foundation from where you can then start to build your own game intelligence.

1. *Find holes in the opponent's defense or formation:* All teams, even the best of the best, have areas where they fall short. Once any weaknesses have been identified, you can attack them with greater confidence, knowing there's more potential for creating goal-scoring opportunities when these weaknesses are exploited effectively.

2. *Watch the ball like a hawk:* Keep a constant eye on the ball and try to anticipate its future path. The ball is ultimately the most important aspect of a soccer game, and the central midfielder is the guardian of it. By keeping tabs on the ball's activity, you will gain a better understanding of where you need to be to intercept it from opponents or receive it from teammates.

3. *Watch opponents collectively and individually*: Keeping one eye constantly on the ball is crucial, but you need to keep the other eye on your opponents. Get to learn their typical movements, identify their weakest foot, and scan their facial expressions and body movements when they are about to make a pass or play. Absorbing details like these can often give away their intentions or reveal their weaknesses, both of which are invaluable to you.

4. *Consider your actions and their successive consequences carefully*: Everything you do affects both your performance and that of the team as a whole. For instance, by moving forward to attack at the wrong time could leave your defense wide open. If the opposition keeps possession of the ball, then they've just been given a goal scoring opportunity on a plate. Thinking-ahead and evaluating each situation quickly, but carefully, will give you a great advantage in any game.

5. *Be an unpredictable attacker*: Vary your runs and your passing techniques. Be consistent in your unpredictable behavior and you will get to confuse the rival side. This will make you more difficult to handle and track by the opposing players.

Improving game intelligence takes time, experience, and a fair amount of trial and error. Even so, this is still something that is well worth pursing as it will lift your game up to a whole new level.

Not only is game intelligence an incredibly effective tool to have in your skills arsenal, but it can be tremendous fun too, once you get good at it.

Furthermore, game intelligence can compensate for a lack of skill or technique in other areas, as well as complement those skills you have already mastered well.

Finally, game intelligence will improve your ability to physically last the duration of games with consistent performance.

This is because you will be able to conserve energy better by playing smarter instead of playing unnecessarily harder.

Intelligent players prove time and again that it isn't always physical skill or pace that makes a soccer player great.

First touch is the key

Another vital asset for central midfielders is to have good technical control of the ball, and the most necessary aspect of this is having a good first touch.

Having an excellent first touch allows midfielders to quickly move the ball into spaces away from opponents.

The first touch approach can often give the midfielder more time to think about what he wants to do with the ball next.

He gets these extra few seconds because so little time has been wasted in controlling and setting up the ball.

Having the ability to do something useful with the ball when using the first touch approach is what enables an offensively-minded central midfielder like Andres Iniesta (the FC Barcelona and Spain national team's central midfielder), to take control of the game as he so often does.

Whether you are already a central midfielder or plan to become one at some point in the future, you need to constantly practice and develop the first touch skill.

This really is fundamental to your success in this position.

Below are some useful tips to that will help guide you with your training.

1. *Always aim to get the ball under your control quickly*: This means you must bring the ball under control and place it where you want in relation to your body using a single touch/movement. In high-pressure, high-tempo games, there just isn't the time to take two or more touches of the ball in an attempt to get it under control and then set it up for the next move. Allowing opponents too much time to close in will only increase the risk of you losing possession of the ball. Any touches after the first touch should be used to dribble or pass the ball on.

2. *Use the first touch to place the ball in a good position, preferably away from opposition players.* If you are ready to take control of the ball but are not completely sure what you should do with it next, then always move toward your own goal in these situations. This conservative method will ensure you don't lose possession of the ball unnecessarily, plus it allows you more time to figure out what your next move should be. Don't become complacent though. Just because you're in a safer area, that doesn't mean you opponents aren't trying to anticipate you next moves.

3. *Use your body to shield the ball from opponents.* Once you have decided where you want to position the ball on the first touch, your next move is to then shield it from opponents. This approach allows you to keep possession of the ball relatively safely while you prepare yourself for the next move.

4. *Sometimes your first touch might need to be a pass.* This is often the case if your team is being pressed hard by the opposition. Instantly passing the ball on reduces the amount of time you have to control it yourself. In these situations, your first touch should be used to prepare the ball for your teammate. Try to direct the ball into an area where the receiving player will have time do something more useful with it.

5. *Follow through*: Once you have made a decision about what to do on the first touch, make sure you follow through on that decision without delay. Hesitance and indecision usually leads to mistakes and a loss of possession, so be sure to act fast.

6. *Shooting on the first touch*: There will be occasions when that first touch calls for an immediate shot. If space and opportunity presents itself, then go for it. First-time shots or volleys can totally surprise the opposing defense and goalkeeper, often resulting in a goal scoring opportunity or a direct goal.

Playing on the first touch is an essential part of your game. Therefore, you need to place a lot of focus on improving this area.

Get good at first touch soccer and you will see your game improve dramatically.

One simple, yet very effective way to practice your first-touch skills is by kicking a ball against a wall and then attempt to control it on the rebounds.

Make sure you start to implement the strategies above when you next have the opportunity to use your first touch skills in practice sessions and games.

Six ways to keep it simple

Are you awestruck and perplexed by some of the complicated, multi-step plays that you see on the soccer field?

Maybe such moves have inspired you to spend more time learning your own fancy footwork and sensational passes, so that you too can become super impressive on the field?

While complex plays can be great to witness, and huge morale boosters when executed effectively, they should not be the focus of a central midfielder's development. In this position, it is the simpler plays which are the nuts and bolts of a central midfielder's game.

Below are six areas in soccer generally, and the central midfield position specifically, where simple, strong play can make all the difference.

1. *Short distance passing*: While a 40-yard cross is impressive, the short simple passes are usually more effective in most situations. Furthermore, they are less likely to be intercepted by the opposing team. In brief, a short pass has less chance of failing and more chance of succeeding. Keep your passes as short and as straightforward as possible and you will maintain more accuracy and better results overall.

2. *Reading the game*: Although a lot of the central midfielder's effort and time is spent trying to anticipate and counteract the actions of his opponents, all you really need to know are these two things: One, where the ball is currently, and two, where is it likely to be in a few seconds. If you have possession of the ball, the actions of the other players on the field are irrelevant at that moment. At these times you don't need to worry about reading the game so much as reading the ball.

3. *Effective communication*: Whether you are communicating with your teammates vocally, through gestures, or by meaningful looks, be sure to keep all communication short and simple. This way you will reduce your opponent's ability to figure out what messages you are conveying. The less they can figure out what your next actions are likely to be, the better it is for you and your team.

4. *Closing loopholes*: Although it is easy to get overwhelmed when your team is under an aggressive attack, the best plan of action is a rather straightforward one. Simply find places where the opposing team can break through and close them up one by one. If you close down the holes in your defense quickly, then your opponents will run out of options. This is one rare occasion where you want to look at details rather than the bigger picture.

5. *Create threatening situations*: As a central midfielder, you will be most effective if you put the majority of your efforts into creating threatening situations for the opposition. The closer these situations are to their goal, the better. Instead of focusing on making the big score, reduce your stress and improve your chances of winning by keeping your attention firmly on creating opportunities to score.

6. *Moving the ball forward*: Moving the ball forward is yet another of those plays where a simple strategy proves to be the easiest and most effective option. Whenever in doubt, always move the ball forwards. This action not only lowers the chance of your opponents scoring, but it also increases your side's potential to score. Keeping the ball moving in a forward direction helps to create a winning situation.

It might seem like there's a lot to consider in the above six points, but the main thing to remember is to focus on simple, easy to execute plays, and ones which have a high chance of succeeding.

When playing as a central midfielder, you are the most important player besides the goalie. It is crucial that you keep a long list of useful data in the forefront of your mind at all times.

This way, you get to evaluate the opposing team effectively, and then turn your quick thinking into fast actions by developing a good, operational game strategy around your judgments. Again, try not to focus on the micro details of a situation, nor look for elaborate maneuvers. Always keep things simple when you can.

Do this by opting for easy–to-execute plays. This will not only make your job much easier but it will also make you a more effective player, thus increasing your chance of succeeding in the process.

He shoots, he scores

Anyone who plays, or is hoping to play as a central midfielder, needs to be incredibly fit and have the stamina to participate in just about every offensive action made by the team.

Because so many players rely on their central midfielders, having good ball skills and a honed sense of precision are absolute must-have qualities.

A central midfielder is the distribution center of the team. He must take the ball and move it to the forwards at every opportunity. Whenever the ball ends up in the defensive third, central midfielders must work with their defenders to regain control of it.

Central midfielders are masters of intimidation, pressuring opponents until they lose their wits (and hopefully the ball in the process). A well-trained central midfielder can scare the opposition out of the way as they take the ball down the field.

With such an imposing presence and impressive list of attributes, it's hard to understand why so many central midfielders lose their nerve when they get close to the goal box, as they so often do.

Every soccer fan has seen a scenario similar to this: the central midfielder fearlessly claims the ball. He then successfully takes it across the field, approaches the goal and then..., passes it on to someone else.

Situations like this can be a huge let down, and usually a strategic mistake as well.

When it comes to scoring goals, even a moment's hesitation is often enough to give the goalie a heads-up, thus allowing him to prepare himself better for what's about to come.

Don't let this all too common mannerism become a part of you and your game. You cannot be apprehensive when it comes to shooting. There just isn't the time to think about alternative options when there's an open opportunity to score.

Anticipating a potentially negative outcome before it's even happened is a recipe for failure.

The way a lot of central midfielders have overcome their hesitance to fire at the goal is to stop thinking and start doing.

That's it in a nutshell. For those who can't or won't break this bad habit for whatever reason continue to give up on almost every scoring opportunity.

These guys might still be really good central midfielders, apart from this reluctance to shoot, but they will never be great players if they don't get rid of this hesitancy at the goalmouth.

Every shot is a possible score, so logic suggests that the more a player shoots the more goals he will score.

It's a simple numbers game. If you are a central midfielder suffering from a shooting anxiety, then try not to think too much and just start doing.

If you would like a bit more guidance than the "don't think, do" approach, then here are three other ways that will surely help you to get over this reluctance to fire shots directly at the goal:

1. *Work on shooting skills during practice sessions:* The more practice you get in between games, the more comfortable and skilled you will become. This is what practice sessions are all about, so make sure you use them to hone in on your shooting. The best thing about practice sessions is that everything is far less stressful, making this the perfect place to overcome any fears and to build confidence.

2. *Make it a policy to shoot at every opportunity:* Just for one game, that's all, make the decision to shoot at every possible chance you get. Don't even think about the possible outcome before taking any of these shots either. If you think too much, reluctance will return. Later on, after the game has long finished and you have had time to relax, compare your performance to other times where you hesitated to shoot. Even if you didn't score from this trial attempt, you will still probably notice two important things, one, you enjoyed yourself a lot more and two, You realize that you had been worrying about nothing for all this time. You will probably then notice how the fear of shooting has been completely removed by this simple one-off exercise.

3. *Faking out the goalie*: You are more likely to shoot if you know the goalie isn't onto you. Being able to trick the keeper of your real intentions will make you more confident and therefore more successful in your shooting attempts.

Approaching the goal box with a soccer ball at your feet can be an intimidating experience. The pressure is certainly on as you brazen out the glares of a stern looking goalie surrounded by his equally stony-faced defenders.

Although it's easy to back away from situations like these, the only real path to success, on most occasions, is to fire a well-aimed shot at the goal.

As you begin to think less and shoot more, you will start to gain a new confidence. Consequently, your shooting skills will improve with each fresh attempt to score, thus adding yet another crucial skill to your already expansive central midfielder arsenal of abilities.

Staying in position

The central midfielder is the team strategist, working effectively between the offense and the defense. From his station in the center of the field, he can see what needs to be done in order to move the team toward a successful outcome. His role is to then rally the players together and work toward this end.

As you can see, this is a key position which carries a lot of influence on the outcome of a game. However, there is one trap that seems to ensnare so many otherwise talented central midfielders, and that is chasing the ball to the far-flung ends of the field.

It is not uncommon to see central midfielders make this mistake; even some professionals do it. The reason this style of play is a mistake is because central midfielders generally serve the team much better when they remain in their position.

Below are the reasons why it's not a good idea for a central midfielder to chase the ball away from his position:

- *It takes him away from the place where he is most needed*: As a central midfielder you need to be accessible to both your team's forwards and your team's defense. Moving too far from the center of the midfield will make this almost impossible. Although you should be mobile and go after the ball whenever it is feasible, you shouldn't play as though you are the only one on the field able to pursue it. Give the other players a chance to perform their duties from their own domains.

- *It affects your ability to see and evaluate the field*: Moving away from your position means temporarily giving up one of your key advantages. From the center of the midfield, where a central midfielder should be by definition, you have a unique viewpoint. You can usually see and evaluate almost every player in the game from this part of the field. It allows you to function as the "brain" of your team. So by leaving your position too often or for too long, you lose this exclusive benefit.

- *Missing key opportunities*: Before leaving your area to chase the ball, you should ask yourself whether it might come back your way anytime soon, and if so, when exactly might that be? After all, you don't want to miss a key opportunity all because you took off and chased the ball into a domain other than your own.

- *Falling prey to an opponent's trap*: Because your position is so important to your team's success, a smart opponent might try to lure you away from your area so that it becomes completely unmanned. Once you're too far away to respond from your official position on the field, the opponents can then proceed with an attack.

When central midfielders contemplate their options, they often find it difficult trying to determine whether the ball is too far away for them to pursue, or whether they should just go after it regardless.

What happens in these decision making moments is that the central midfielder makes a relatively straightforward situation unnecessarily complicated. And whenever anything becomes complicated, it then becomes harder to be effective.

Having a few hard and fast rules - and sticking by those rules no matter what - will help you to reinforce a more structured style of play. This will then prevent you from spontaneously straying into areas of the game that are not supportive to you or your team.

Here are a few simple pointers that will help you to avoid falling into this trap of chasing after the ball.

First and foremost, never ever lose sight of the ball. At every moment of the game you should be conscious of where the ball is and who is in possession of it.

The second point to consider is to always try and predict where the ball will be taken next, and more importantly, when will it likely enter your domain and what do you plan to do with it when it does?

Thinking in this way, two-steps ahead of the game, gives you the ability to step in quickly and decisively when the opportunity presents itself.

Whenever chasing the ball is not a reasonable option, as it won't be most of the time, just focus on other central midfielder key functions like closing down all possible options for your opponents to break through.

Just as a goalie should be cautious and justified when leaving his goal box, so should a central midfielder whenever he decides to leave his domain and go tearing after the ball into territories other than his own.

You might also want to note that while every sector of the field has a teammate ready to overtake the ball, no one can really take your place as a central midfielder.

Therefore, it is better that you, the playmaker, is always at home to defend that very important zone in front of your team's defense.

Defensive Midfielder (DM) – The Heart of The Team

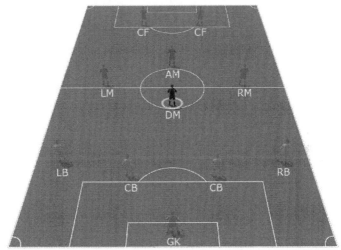

The defensive midfielder is a complex position, and you have to be a complex player to perform well in this role.

Although defensive midfielders seem to have a seemingly simple mission on the face of it, that being to defend their goal by keeping opponents as far away as possible, they also have to back up other players.

There are times, in fact, when they are required to take on almost every other defensive or midfielder role in the game.

Having this type of versatility requires more than just a player who is willing to adapt his game to meet the needs of the team. He must also possess a variety of technical skills along with a strong mindset.

What is a defensive midfielder?

The defensive midfielder is basically a one-man dam, holding opponents away from the team's goal.

They have a diverse range of skills at their disposal which they use to keep their attackers back. However, their responsibilities don't end with this one task as you are about to find out.

As mentioned in the introduction, a defensive midfielder also backs up other players such as other midfielders and fullbacks, and even direct defensive players.

You will be moving from sideline to sideline doing whatever it takes to take possession of the ball, whether that's tackling opponents or making supporting runs.

Essential skills

The most essential skill for succeeding as a defensive midfielder is stamina. No other player is required to cover quite as much ground as a defensive midfielder, and that means there's a lot of running around to do a lot of the time.

It has been estimated that a defensive midfielder runs an average of 12 kilometers in every game. Even so, it's not only stamina and the ability to run a good distance that is required of these guys.

The role also entails receiving and passing the ball constantly, so a defensive midfielder must also have superior passing skills and a solid first touch.

Tackling is another must-have skill, just as it is in every other defensive position.

Essential personality traits

Defensive midfielders need to be mentally strong as well technically superior. This is a perfect position for someone who possesses natural leadership skills and the ability to inspire others.

Anyone looking to play in this position must know that they will not only be executing plays themselves, but also directing other players to help them out as and when necessary.

The role also involves encouraging the team in difficult or discouraging moments during a game. It's therefore no coincidence that the defensive midfielder is often assigned the job of team captain.

Although leadership is an important trait it's not as important as effective teamwork.

Defensive midfielders must be equally able to give assistance to the other players when they most need it, and also let them have their moment in the spotlight.

Benefits and drawbacks

One of the benefits of the defensive midfielder position is that it sees a lot of action. That makes this a great job for anyone who likes to be in the thick of the game.

Another advantage is that this position gives players a chance to use a variety of moves in every single game, thus helping them to maintain their wide range of skills.

One very important drawback that you need to think about before jumping into this position is the fact that you will rarely have an opportunity to actually score goals yourself.

Although you will play an integral part to every single score made by the team, you will still miss out on some of the glory that other players get to bask in.

Despite the lack of goal scoring opportunities, the defensive midfielder is by no means a "behind the scenes" position.

It's a job that can be extremely rewarding for the right person. This is an action packed position, and one which is crucial to the overall success of the team.

Should you play as defensive midfielder?

The ideal defensive midfielder is someone who's a complex and well-rounded individual.

Yes he needs to be clever with the ball, but it's not only good physical skills that he requires.

A defensive midfielder should be a born leader too; someone who can delegate as well as he can play.

He has both long-lasting stamina and the ability to produce short bursts of intense speed when it's required of him.

Although fitting into the shoes of a defensive midfielder is a tall order, many dedicated players who didn't initially have what was required of the role, then went on to master the skills and develop the traits necessary to meet the prerequisites.

In other words, they were able to grown themselves into this action-packed and very satisfying position.

The defensive midfielder's dilemma

Variety may be the spice of life, but it is not always the welcome spice of a defensive midfielder's game.

All soccer players have an arsenal of complicated plays at their disposal, including defensive midfielders.

However, defensive midfielders often find themselves falling back on the most basic of strategies, namely tackling and passing the ball.

Perhaps one of the most common traps for players in the position of defensive midfielder is getting caught up in transporting the ball.

In the majority of these cases, they would have been better off passing the ball on to another teammate.

There are several reasons to avoid transporting the ball when playing in the position of defensive midfielder.

Firstly, while there are many soccer positions dedicated to moving the ball from Point A to Point B, the role of a defensive midfielder does not usually involve this.

A defensive midfielder usually has enough on his plate as it is, with things like breaking up the opposing team's attacks and backing up his defensive players.

Therefore, it makes more sense for him to focus his efforts on tackling, and passing the ball on quickly.

Once he's completed his moves he must always make sure he returns to his defensive position whenever he's strayed from his domain. This brings us to the second point.

Transporting the ball takes the player far away from the opposing team's offense.

Needless to say that this makes him unavailable if the action returns quickly to his part of the field.

So the best tactic for a defensive midfielder is to stay in his position at all times and let the forwards focus on moving the ball toward the goal.

The defensive midfielder has more important matters to attend to, like strategically positioning himself so that he's there, willing and able to interfere with the opponent's next inevitable attack.

The third reason why it's a bad idea for a defensive midfielder to use his valuable time and energy transporting the ball is that it can be both distracting and confusing.

This is because defensive midfielders must have good intuition. For this to be effective they have to be aware of the movements of the players around them.

Taking the ball up and down the field reduces the defensive midfielder's ability to pay close attention to the rhythm of the game, and when this happens he's unable to discern where he will be needed next.

This obviously compromises and even completely undermines his position. In short, he becomes a hindrance rather than a help to his side because of his decision to run with the ball.

Another thing to consider is the energy aspect.

Getting caught up in transporting the ball repeatedly throughout the game will result in the defensive midfielder using up his valuable energy reserves unnecessarily, and before the game is over.

An exhausted player loses both his physical and his mental enthusiasm, something else that will lessen his value to the team.

So if you are, or you hope to become, a defensive midfielder on your team, then do yourself a favor and don't ever get tempted or caught up in transporting the ball for any real distance.

You will see enough action in every game as it is, without having to do this.

Removing yourself from your position, and draining your valuable energy supplies unnecessarily in the process, will only serve to damage your overall effectiveness.

So stand your ground, defend "your territory," and quickly pass that ball over to one of your teammates who will be eagerly waiting to receive it.

Your team needs you; they depend on you to be their kingpin, and you can't be that when you're running off in all directions with the ball.

Some of the best soccer players in the world are, and have been, defensive midfielders.

These star players are the ones who stand their ground and never stray far, never allowing holes to form in the defense from where the opposing team can break through.

Staying in your position will help create not just a more effective defense, but a more specialized team with less confusion about duties and roles.

Passing, instead of getting involved in transporting the ball, will make both you and your team a much stronger side.

Just remember the crucial points above, heed the traps, and you will develop the good habits necessary to be a consistent and successful defensive midfielder.

Dealing with chatter on the midfield

Yackety yak, yackety yak! If this is sounding less like the 1958 classic pop song, and more like your opponents, then it's time to come up with a few ways of dealing with the inevitable and distracting banter that often inflicts the game of soccer.

The midfield is a crowded area where intimidation and even outright bullying are common strategies, especially by a losing opposition.

As unpleasant as this can be, it is still something that you will have to learn to deal with if you want to be successful in the position of defensive midfielder.

Inexperienced defensive midfielders can find themselves getting quite flustered and distracted at times by their opponents' verbal taunts.

Without having any kind of plan for dealing with this type of behavior, the opponent's strategy works, as they hoped it would do.

What happens when verbal tactics are used as an intimidation tool is that the one being intimidated can lose his ability to play effectively.

That is the whole point.

So if this happens to you, then it may feel as though the game is slipping away from under you, despite your best efforts to push on and ignore the taunting.

When this happens, the harasser gets to relish in his achievement, beating you in every move as you become less and less effective in your role.

The good news is that it doesn't have to be like this.

There are a few strategies that other defensive midfielders have used to deal with this verbal taunting and with great results too.

Below are just a few of these winning actions that will surely help you too if you're in need of a lifeline on how to deal with the midfield chatter.

- *Focus totally on the game*: Find specific focus to occupy your mind such as concentrating on the ball at all times. This will not only improve your play, but it will also give you something to think about other than the nearby, loud-mouthed opponent. By watching the ball as it moves around the field, trying to predict what will happen next, and how you might exploit the situation, will definitely help you to become less aware, if not totally oblivious to any verbal distraction that's going on around you.

- *Ignore insults*: Although it can be hard not to take these gibes seriously, remember that your opponent is simply grasping at straws. Insults are the last ditch ploys of a player who knows he has nothing else to offer. Try to view insulting remarks as a sign of desperation. This will help you to maintain your calm by keeping any unpleasant comments in proper perspective.

- *Never engage in banter.* While it can be tempting to hit back with an equally snappy response to a provocative remark, just know that doing this will only put you on the same low level as the opponent. Instead, just smile to yourself and refuse categorically to get dragged in to the tormenter's game. This will not only keep you from getting flustered and distracted, but it will most likely have a reverse affect to what the opponent had hoped for. You see, whenever you don't take the bait in these situations, the plan then turns back on the instigator. He then ends up as the one who's distracted and upset; annoyed at you for not responding to his strategy. Seriously, there is nothing more frustrating to a jibing opponent than a player who refuses to argue back.
- *Prove them wrong by winning.* If you cannot help feeling upset by an opponent constantly talking into your ears, then channel this discontent into better plays and enhanced accuracy. Use your annoyance as a tool to boost your energy and incentive, and to make every play count. In other words, prove to your opponent that his attempts to provoke are not only wasted but actually helping you to play better. Do this by displaying positive actions as opposed to negative reactions. This approach works really well for some individuals so you might want to give it try.

- *Be the better player and the better person:*

You already know that you are physically and intellectually superior to a player who prefers to hurl out inflammatory remarks rather than focus his energies into playing the game.

When you remind yourself of this simple fact whenever playing in a chatter- packed midfield, it will lift you above all the taunts.

If anything, you will be able to play with even more confidence and skill once you acknowledge your superior position over that of the jibing opponent.

It can be difficult for an inexperienced player to cope with too much distracting banter on the field.

However, because this is something that is unavoidable, to a greater or lesser extent, you must learn to deal with it.

Using some of the techniques above will definitely help you to keep your spirits high and your focus firmly on the game.

Once you can put this provocative method in perspective, knowing that it's not personal, but tactical, albeit a bad, unfair tactic, then you will definitely get to grow a thicker skin and rise above it all.

With a little knowledge, practice, and experience, blocking out all that background chatter will become second nature to you, much to the detriment of those who use such underhanded tactics of distraction.

Skills needed for a defensive midfielder

If you're still wondering if you have what it takes to play as your team's defensive midfielder, then keep reading because there's more to consider.

This position is vital to a team's defense specifically, and to the team's overall success more broadly.

Below are the top 10 skills required for being a successful defensive midfielder:

1. *Pass first, dribble second*: As a defensive midfielder, the general rule is to always pass first and dribble second. This is because dribbling will rarely get you far in this position. Therefore, you will need to know how to pass quickly and accurately if you're to succeed in this role.

2. *Pursuing the ball*: As a defensive midfielder, you should spend much of your game moving laterally across the field, relentlessly pursuing the ball. Just your presence can make the opposition's forwards nervous, making them more prone to mistakes as a consequence.

3. *Providing backup*: If a midfield teammate is beaten, the defensive midfielder's job is to step in and save the day. This ensures there are no holes in the defense for the opposition to exploit.

4. *Keeping the opposition away from the goal*: This can be done either by pushing them toward the flanks or forcing them back. Either way, an offensive player who is nowhere near the ball or the goal is not going to be able to score or make any other plays that could change the course of the game.

5. *Tackling is essential*: Whenever an opponent is moving in on your goal, tackling becomes an essential skill. You, as the defensive midfielder, need to move in quickly, take possession of the ball, and then attempt to move it back to the other side of the field where it belongs.

6. *Intimidation and anxiety*: A defensive midfielder can become an impressive and imposing presence on the field. Being able to give off an aura of intimidation can make it hard for the opposition to relax. Anxiety leads to mistakes and mistakes from the opposition lead to more scoring opportunities for your team.

7. *Marking is really important*: This is one of the most essential defensive skills, so it's obviously a must-have talent for defensive midfielders. Quite often your position is assigned to marking the opposing team's best forward, so you need to take this skill very seriously.

8. *Teamwork is crucial*: A defensive midfielder must be a real team player. This is not a position for those who seek a little self-glory and accolades. A defensive midfielder should never have the ball for too long. His primary role is to quickly transfer possession of it to his forwards.

9. *Anticipation gives you an immense advantage*: Any player can tell you where the ball is at any moment in time, but it takes an experienced defensive midfielder to tell you where the ball will be in a few seconds time. Having this type of intuition will give you a huge advantage because it avoids making false starts and running around unnecessarily.

10. *Creativity is an art*: Defensive midfielders are often thrust into impossible situations with confusing demands and lots of pressure. To come up with an action that will save the day takes more than just superior soccer skills; it also takes a high level of creativity. Think of yourself as the Picasso of the playing field.

Read the game and stop the attack

In theory, playing as a defensive midfielder seems simple enough.

After all, defending is basically the act of closing down the opponent's ability to pass, dribble, or score, thus leaving them no option but to eventually turn the ball over to the control of your team.

Like most simple theories, the actual practice is never quite as easy or as straightforward as it might seem.

In order to actually be effective as a defensive midfielder you will need to possess a diverse range of skills and talent.

Below are a few strategies that all good defensive midfielders use in their game.

- *Read your opponents' next move*: Reading an opponent's next move is a lot easier said than it is done, but if you practice you will progress in this area. This is not something which is purely intuitive either. It can be learned just like any other skill can be learned. The secret is to first train your eyes so that you can recognize unusual movements, especially diagonal movements. Players will always be moving up and down the field or from side to side. However, when you see diagonal movements in your opponents, then there is a very good chance they are setting themselves up for an offensive play. Make sure you also watch your opponent's feet very carefully. While players can easily fake their intentions by the clever use of body language, including their eyes and various facial expressions, it is not so easy to mislead with the feet. Players must position their feet in a particular way whenever they're about to pass or receive the ball. So keep your eyes low and you'll always know where the ball is heading to next.

- *Watch the less used players*: Many surprise attacks involve a player who has been underestimated. This is a shockingly common strategy, yet often a very effective one. While you should focus a lot of your time and attention on the most skilled players in the opposing team, make sure you don't only focus on them. If you do, then you can fall for this simple trap whereby the little guys slip past you quite unnoticed, that is until it's too late!
- *Know how offensive players work*: This can be as simple as occasionally studying your own team's offensive players or as complicated as you playing in an offensive position from time to time (recommended). With the latter approach, you get a better overall understanding of the offensive roles, and that can really help in the way you play your usual defensive position. Offensive players have a very different style and therefore a different way of executing plays. So understanding these better will give you a distinct advantage in the role of defensive midfielder.

- *Leave no player unmarked*: One of your key duties as a defensive midfielder is to direct your team's defense in protecting the goal area. The most effective way to do this, in most cases, is to mark the opposing team's forwards in a one-on-one formation. When you assign your strongest player to the opponent with the ball, his options become greatly reduced. This effectively shuts down passing options and inhibits shooting. With little else left for the opponent to do, your team is likely to retake possession of the ball. Effective marking also reduces the chance of a coordinated attack to almost zero.
- *Always be the man with a plan*: Even if you don't have possession of the ball, having a strategy still gives your side an edge. You will be the one who gets to ultimately dictate the path of the ball. Your opponents may make a breakthrough play occasionally, but the most focused team is usually the one that comes out on top. Having a plethora of effective strategies that you can fall back on at a moment's notice is something that will take time, lots of research, and plenty of practical experience.

- *Stay physically fit:* Staying in good shape might seem obvious, but it's not always advice that's heeded among some amateurs. In many soccer games, the winner of duels is not necessarily the most skilled player, but the one who's the most resourceful and fittest. Of course it's important to know a variety of plays and to have great ball handling skills, but success also demands that you have the strength to face down an opponent and the stamina to outlast them.

As you can see, the requirements for playing well as a defensive midfielder can be broken down into a shortlist of specific skills and strategies that can be practiced and developed by anyone who fits the profile.

Attacking/Offensive Midfielder (AM/OM) – The Wings of The Team

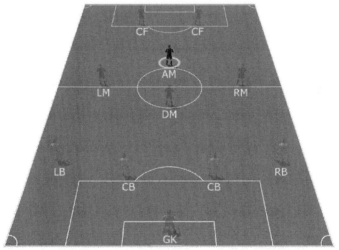

If you are interested in becoming an attacking/offensive midfielder, then you need to prepare for the ride of your life.

Strategically placed between the midfield and the strikers, these guys see more action than any other player in the game of soccer.

An attacking/offensive midfielder gets to be a part of some of the most crucial plays in each and every game.

What is an Attacking/Offensive midfielder?

Most soccer players know that an attacking/offensive midfielder plays in the midfield and that he is involved in offensive plays.

However, that is merely a brief introduction into the full job description.

An attacking/offensive midfielder is more specifically involved in scoring goals, and lots of them.

They are the central player around whom the whole offensive game revolves.

On the other hand, an attacking/offensive midfielder not only scores goals, but he's also responsible for creating goal scoring opportunities for his teammates as well.

Because the role of an attacking/offensive midfielder is so important to any soccer team, he is another one those players nicknamed "the playmaker."

This is because of his ability to leads attacks and to bring in other players from the same side to positions from where they too can score.

No other player is as influential as the attacking/offensive midfielder in the success of the offense.

This is all thanks to his ability to both initiate and finish an astonishing number of offensive plays.

Essential skills

If you want to be an attacking/offensive midfielder for your team, then you will need to have a diverse range of skills.

This position requires a number of abilities, especially in areas such as dribbling, passing, shooting, and good ball control in general.

You will also need to be an expert strategist, someone who is able to come up with creative maneuvers quickly and while under immense pressure from the opposition.

Essential personality traits

Skills alone are not enough to win games in this position. You must also possess good mental aptitude too.

For attacking/offensive midfielders, the most important thing of all is to have a complete understanding of the role in its entirety.

In a high-pressure, high-tempo game, it can be very easy to get distracted by all the commotion at times.

Therefore, by fully knowing your place and your specific duties, you will be better able to adhere to the obligations of your role without becoming preoccupied by the unfolding goings-on.

Composure is another key trait for an attacking/offensive midfielder.

Because of your position on the field, you will often find yourself in difficult and intimidating situations. For this reason, having the ability to remain calm and composed is absolutely fundamental to your success.

Possessing good intuition may not be a key trait for the role but it will certainly be a help to you, as with it would with any of the other eleven soccer positions.

So if you lack somewhat in the "intuition department," then you might want to look at developing this further as a secondary skill.

Lastly is creativity. This can be an immense advantage for anyone playing in the position of attacking/offensive midfielder.

Offensive play requires having the ability to get around any obstruction in your path. There are certainly situations where the only way around an obstruction is with some seriously imaginative and very quick thinking.

Because an attacking/offensive midfielder plays an offensive position, a decent measure of courage is also required.

There is nothing quite as intimidating as facing down a goalkeeper, but as an attacking/offensive midfielder you will need to do this frequently. This means being intimidated by the rival goalkeeper is not an option that's open to you.

Similarly, standing up to teammates may often be necessary in this position too, usually when there are conflicts over the best way to carry out a strategy.

Having an ability to rally support from the other players, while keeping hurt feelings to a minimum, is a true sign of leadership. It will never be possible, however, to please all of the players all of the time.

For that reason, developing a thick skin is advisable in this position; something that can also be acquired through practice.

Benefits and drawbacks

The main benefit of being an attacking/offensive midfielder is that you are always right in the middle of the action.

While other players spend the game responding to various plays, you are busy inventing and carrying them out. Despite the seeming excitement associated with this position, there is one potential major drawback to it.

Your role means that you are burdened with a lot of responsibility.

Now if you are someone who thrives under pressure, then that's fine, but if you are someone who cracks when the going gets tough, then this might not be the right position on the field for you, or you may want to reconsider after you've gained more experience on the field.

A major benefit of this position is that is does come with some glory.

Not everyone likes being in the spotlight, but a little fame on the field is what other players live for.

In fact, these types wouldn't even consider playing in a low-key role. For them, the attacking/offensive midfielder is a very attractive position.

The obvious flipside to a high profile position is that when mistakes are made, as they inevitably are from time to time, then the player is also in the spotlight, only this time for all the wrong reasons.

On these occasions his head will be held in shame, rightly or wrongly, as opposed to high and proud.

Situations where the attacking/offensive midfielder makes a complete blunder obviously create the total reverse effect of what a high profile player wants to happen to them.

But hey, if you can't stand the heat, then keep out of the kitchen, as that wise old adage goes.

In other words, one must be able to take the rough with the smooth.

Should you play as attacking/offensive midfielder?

There is a lot of variation in the styles and particular skills sets of players in the position of attacking/offensive midfielder, but they all have a few key traits in common:
-   Excellent technical skills
-   A sharp mind
-   Willingness to play hard for the benefit of the team.

While the role of an attacking/offensive midfielder is one of immense action, it also requires mental resilience and sharp wit.

This can be a tall order, but on most teams there is usually at least one person who can hold up to the challenge.

For a lot of players this position is an attractive one, in theory at least. In practice though, not so many go on to make the job of attacking/offensive midfielder's their permanent position.

Others don't even meet the requirements, despite their best efforts to shine.

It's a demanding role, that's for sure, and it comes with many challenges, so it's obviously not a position which suites everyone.

If you think you might have what it takes to be the attacking/offensive midfielder of your team, of other team looking to fill the position, then the only way to know for sure is to try out for it and then give it a go should you pass the tryout.

The role of attacking midfielders

Attacking midfielders are positioned in the midfield as the name suggests. They are also responsible for both scoring goals and assisting in goal scoring.

This position is part of soccer's foundation. It doesn't matter how good the defense is, no game is won without scoring goals, and that's where the attacking midfielders come into play.

The only way to become a champion goal scorer is to keep shooting. Attacking midfielders attempt shots at the goal with every opportunity that presents itself.

For anyone to be successful in this position, they must have creativity, intelligence, stamina, and of course superior technical skills.

Below are a few of the essential skills that you will need to call on the moment a goal scoring opportunity presents itself.

- *Possessing good ball skills*: Because you will be spending a lot of time with the soccer ball, it is essential to know how to work it effectively.
- *Passing with accuracy*: You are also part of the offensive team, and so one of your duties is to create opportunities for teammates to score. That means giving the ball away at those times when another player is in a better position than you are to take the shot. Such decisions are usually done under pressure and require good accuracy and quick thinking.
- *Shooting to score*: This is where the magic happens and the points are scored. Knowing how to skillfully work a ball around the most alert keeper is an ability that will make you a star, regardless of your other skills and attributes.
- *Run like a dynamo*: You'll be spending a lot of the game running around, so distance abilities are a must-have. You will also need to turn power up for quick runs, so work on sprinting as well. The fastest soccer player on the team is usually the one making all the scores too because everyone else is simply left behind.

- *Dribble with confidence*: While passing is always preferred to dribbling, sometimes you need to get the ball from point A to point B with a lesser risk of interception. This is where you will sometimes appreciate being a fast and tight dribbler.
- *Teamwork, not solo, is the name of the game*: Take note of the line about being "a part of" the offensive team. When you are a part of something, you cannot be apart from it. That means there is no place in this position for going solo. Working well with your teammates by giving them scoring opportunities is the only successful formula. Selfless play not only increases your chances of winning the game, but it also gains you a lot more respect from the other players when you contribute to the broader team effort.
- *Become an authority*: Like any other trait, you can learn how to successfully lead others in a convincing and productive way. An authoritative and commanding attacking midfielder can be an incredibly effective team leader, guiding the offense to score time after time, leading his team to one victory after another. Good leadership really is paramount to the successful outcome of a game.

All these skills combined will make you a shooting, scoring machine, and someone who is feared by the opposition.

As long as you and your offensive team work well together, have strong leadership, and enough confidence, skill, and stamina to carry through to the end, then you have a well-oiled unit in place that will see you victorious more often than not.

Shooting for the stars

As important as defensive play can be, your team cannot, and will not, win a single game without scoring goals.

As an attacking/offensive midfielder, much of the responsibility for scoring these goals falls on your shoulders.

Your teammates are depending on you to back them up as a midfielder and to score as many points as possible as an attacker. The simplest way to meet these needs, and to increase your number of goals, is to increase how often you shoot.

Although it sounds obvious, too many soccer players give up numerous opportunities to shoot.

They do this by either opting out at the very last minute or failing to see opportunities as they emerge.

It is a rare and skilled player who sees opportunities to shoot that others neglect to notice, and then take advantage of every single one, often catching opponents off guard in the process.

If you watch the best attacking midfielders in the world, you will immediately notice how they tend to shoot almost every time the ball lands at their feet.

They have developed the knack of finding a path to the goal that isn't always obvious to most others. Each time they spot one of these openings they never fail to shoot, and those who shoot the most, score the most.

Although shooting as often as possible is the most important principle, that doesn't mean you just kick the ball in the general direction of the goal and hope for the best.

Every shot has to have real potential, otherwise there's no point to it. In fact, it can backfire if it isn't calculated.

So shoot as often as you can, but only when you can see a real possibility for a successful outcome.

Firing at the goal is the end result of your efforts, it's the thing you do after all else. So let's now take a look at a few other soccer skills that are required, the ones that lead up to your scoring attempts.

- *Predicting the game*: It can be difficult to make a sound decision the split second a ball touches your foot. This is why it is so important to watch the game carefully and know exactly what you plan to do if and when the ball comes your way.

- *Use your teammates*: You won't be bringing the ball down the field by yourself, and this is why a good working relationship with your teammates is so crucial. Working well with others will not only give you the opportunity to shoot more often, but it will also allow you to safely move the ball from player to player when shooting is not an option.

- *Ball handling skills*: It is equally important to have superior ball handling skills. These are needed so that you can execute your plans quickly and accurately, thus allowing you to take every opportunity to shoot and score.
- *Develop your stamina*: While many people don't really look at stamina as a skill, it actually is. Like other soccer skills, stamina must be practiced and worked on regularly in order to develop it. You need to get to the point where you have all the energy needed to carry you through a game from start to finish. This is the skill that keeps your physical and mental game switched on. Anyone who is physically and mentally prepared is much more likely to succeed than those who are not. When the opposition around you begins to tire your stamina will prove invaluable.
- *Develop your shooting skills*: Although this seems overly obvious, too many players stop working on their shooting once they think they've reached a peak. This is a very bad idea. Not only is there always room for more improvements, but failing to maintain existing skills through regular practice could actually see them weaken. For as long as you play competitive soccer you should always be looking for new drills, new skills, and new methods of getting the ball past the goalkeeper.

- *Shooting over... and over.* Statistics prove that the more a player shoots, the more he scores. It's just simple logic really. Furthermore, by shooting at every given opportunity you will gain more confidence, become more experienced, and inevitably learn new techniques in the process. Hesitancy, on the other hand, will have a reverse effect.

If you work on these skills, and any others that you feel are standing between you and an incredible scoring record, then you are certain to see a rapid improvement in your personal performance and also that of your team.

Just remember this simple fact: without taking the shot, there can be no goal.

The only way to lead your team to victory is to keep firing well-aimed balls at the goalmouth, and to continue working tirelessly on improving your existing skills still further.

Following through with your attack

The role of an attacking/offensive midfielder is a simple one. His job is to score goals and to create scoring opportunities for others on the team.

Whenever a game is clean, and that means being played by the rules, the tasks of an attacking/offensive midfielder can be relatively simple, not least because he is often one of the most skilled and confident players on the side.

So when everything is going according to plan, the attacking/offensive midfielder knows exactly what he needs to do and so he just gets on and does it.

However, not all games go according to plan, in fact very few games are straightforward for all kinds of reasons.

This means that there are several pitfalls that can and do befall even the most confident and skillful of players, distraction being one of the top hazards.

Too many attacking/offensive midfielders become sidetracked and let their guard down when they're near the goal area.

These distractions can cause hesitancy and make both you and the players around you, more vulnerable. Below are a few of the pitfalls to watch out for when distraction takes over.

1. *It gives the opposing defensive players an opportunity to tackle or intercept the ball.* Your key objective is to score or to quickly set up a scoring opportunity for another player. This should be your primary focus in all situations. So avoid holding back or performing other plays whenever you're in front of the goal area.

2. *It brings you to the attention of the goalie:* Goalkeepers tend to be highly intelligent and very good at predicting behavior. The longer they get to watch you in front of their goal area, the more likely they are to figure out what it is you're planning to do next. This puts the keeper in a much better position to stop your plan from succeeding.

3. *Waiting to shoot is tempting fate*: Although it's possible that waiting to shoot in certain situations may produce a better outcome, this is usually not the case. Most players avoid shooting because they are intimidated by the circumstances or they are afraid of failing in a highly visible way. To become a successful attacking/offensive midfielder, waiting is not generally in your list of options.

4. *The more you shoot the more you score*: This is a simple, statistical fact, and something that should be etched into the forefront of your mind. Understand too that knowledge without action is worthless. Whether your offensive strategy is to take the shot yourself or pass the ball over a teammate so that he can score, you should always do everything in your power to keep that ball firing toward the opponent's goal.

Anxiety is something that keeps many players from shooting at that crucial moment.

Even at times when scoring seems highly likely, anxiety can still make a player reluctant to even try.

This fear of potential failure has to go if you're to succeed in the position of an attacking/offensive midfielder.

Below are a few ways where you can maximize the potential of every shot's success, and thus raise confidence in your ability to play well.

More confidence means more success and more success means less fear. The cycle of anxiety and hesitancy can be broken with a little willingness to change.

1. *Watch the game closely. Constantly be on the lookout for potential opportunities:* Having this constant awareness will prepare you better for when the ball comes your way.
2. *Plan your shot before the ball comes your way:* No one has time to think once they have the ball, so make sure you have a plan of action before it even lands at your feet.
3. *Whether high or low, make the goalie work:* If you have to shoot under pressure, make sure the goalie has to move quickly in his attempt to block the ball. The more he has to jump, the more likely he is to make a mistake that hopefully leads to a score for your team.
4. *When in doubt, fire the shot:* Shooting must always have preference over passing and other non-scoring plays. Once you get used to firing well-aimed shots at the opponent's goal, it will become second nature.

An attack is only as good as its finish, so follow through with your plan despite any anxiety or shortcomings you have, or think you have.

In most cases, this means taking the shot. You may surprise yourself by scoring many more goals than you would have ever thought possible.

Even if you miss, which is the very worst case scenario, and certainly not life-threatening, just accept the failed outcome and learn from it.

Look for ways of building new, more effective strategies. Sometimes, self-improvement can come about simply by not repeating an action that didn't work previously.

Learning from your failed attempts will teach you far more than your successful ones ever could do, so never be afraid to fail; failure is your friend.

Double your advantage by using both feet

Having the ability to use both of your feet equally, or as near to equal as you can achieve, is a skill that will set you apart from the rest.

This is a trait which you often find in top attacking midfielders.

Players who can switch to either foot when the situation warrants it have a unique advantage over their opponents. In fact, it almost doubles their potential to succeed in many situations.

Any player who can control, pass, cross, and shoot the ball using either side of his body is undoubtedly more of an asset to his team that one-footed players.

The reason why most soccer players are one-footed is because using both feet can be an incredibly difficult skill to master.

In fact, this is not something that everyone can grasp, despite their best efforts to develop the weaker foot.

This ability is often a naturally latent skill which some players pick up with remarkable ease whereas others just can't seem to get it.

In most cases though, the majority of committed players can become better at using both their feet providing they are patient and persistent in their efforts.

Even though some players will never become truly proficient with their weaker foot, they can still get to a point where they can use it to get them out of tight spots.

This is something they weren't always able to do, so even a limited use of the weaker foot is better than no use at all.

When it comes to improving your non-prominent side, the first step is to simply start using your weaker foot as much as possible.

Getting a feeling for it will lay the foundation for further development.

The secret here is to keep mindful of what you're trying to achieve, and to make sure you force yourself to use the weaker foot in training and in friendly/practice games.

Your natural instinct will always be to use your strong side, and so you will have to fight against this in the beginning.

Providing you stick to your plan, you will definitely start to see your weaker foot strengthen over time, and as it does, your mind will become more comfortable with the idea.

Once the brain and the body start working with you, as opposed to against you, as will be the case in the early days, then you are truly on the path to developing this extremely useful skill.

Below are a few areas where being able to use both feet is a priceless advantage:

1. *Dribbling your opponents*: Being able to dribble with both feet will allow you to fool your opponents more easily. You will be skilled at shifting the ball onto either foot, thus enabling you to move more freely and unpredictably as a consequence. Your opponent will quickly learn that you are two-footed and will find it much harder to predict your movements and stifle your game. He will not be happy!

2. *Passing and receiving*: You maneuver your body less when receiving or passing the ball. This is because you are now able to work comfortably with either foot. This also gives you a little extra time to think, which in turn allows you to play more confidently and fluidly, thus helping you to avoid making awkward movements to get out of tricky situations. Your actions on the field will also be less predictable to your opponents. Having the ability keep them guessing about which side you will use next is an invaluable asset to you.

3. *Being able to shoot the ball with power and accuracy using either foot is a special advantage*: An attacking midfielder who is only one-footed is encumbered by the fact that he must constantly have the ball at his prominent foot before striking it. This reduces his goal-scoring potential dramatically. Furthermore, the switch gives the opposing defender more time to get in a challenge. The opposition defense and goalkeeper will often attempt to force a one-footed player to use his weaker foot, giving him no option but to shoot with it, or at least try to shoot with it. Two-footed attacking midfielders, on the other hand, are entirely unpredictable to the opposition and far more versatile in their ability to finish well.

Useful exercises that can help to strengthen your weaker foot include setting up cones to dribble around, making sure you only use the foot you wish to improve.

You can also have a shooting practice session whereby you only use your weaker side to strike the ball.

Also, try to play Keepy Uppy with your weaker foot and combine it with passing practice with either a friend or a teammate.

Just know that the more you work with your weaker foot, the more your weaker foot will work for you.

Left/Right Midfielder (LM/RM) - The Speedy Gonzales

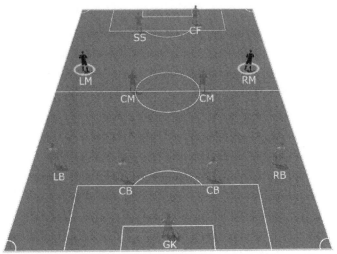

If you are looking for a soccer position that offers excitement and action throughout the entire game, then the left or right midfielder job may be just what you're looking for.

Located far to the right or the left of the center third of the field, these players are responsible for moving the ball from one side of the field to the other, often with a pack of enthusiastic opponents hot on their heels.

Because of their positions, they are often called wide midfielders. The "left" and "right" designation simply refers to what side the player is assigned to and which foot they play with.

In order to do well as a left or right midfielder you must play extremely well in high-pressured situations. That means game consistency and stamina are crucial attributes.

If you're wondering whether you have what is required for playing in the position of a left or right midfielder, then take at the items below.

This list looks at some of the fundamental areas that have to be developed before anyone can be seriously considered for the role.

- *Work on stamina regularly*: Your basic role in the team requires you to run up and down the wings of the field, chasing the ball and working tirelessly to move it to your forwards. Running out of steam is simply not an option. Some players have natural stamina whereas others have to work at developing it. Many find that distance running is a good way to build up stamina.

- *Improve your speed*: When you are needed on the field, you will be needed immediately. This requires the ability to move quicker than any other player, and at a moment's notice. Sprinting and other aerobic activities that require intense bursts of energy are all good for developing this kind of quick response.

- *Practice your ball skills*: Left and right midfielder positions require you to move the soccer ball swiftly and accurately. This means you will need an effective first touch, dribbling skills to get the ball quickly from A-B, and the ability to pass and cross with precision and speed. There are several drills that practice these skills, but simply kicking the ball around with teammates is often a good place to start. Although you will spend much of your time without the ball, your handling of it when it does come your way will be crucial to the outcome of the game.
- *Avoid the middle of the field*: Although there is a huge temptation to go where the action is (usually the middle of the field), you generally serve your team best interest by staying on the flanks. You may feel exiled at times, but that is just something that comes with the territory (all soccer positions have at least a couple of minus points to them). You still have plenty to do though, even when you don't have possession of the ball, things like closing down holes in your midfield, which in turn closes down openings and options for the opposing team.

-   *Take care of yourself.* Obviously you can't play at your best if you physically neglect yourself. Nor can you hope to turn up and perform at your best after burning the candles at both ends (something too many amateurs try, much to their detriment of themselves and the team). Make sure you are properly nourished, hydrated, and well-rested before every single game. Midfielders, more so than any other players, need to be relaxed and refreshed so that they can give their physical and emotional all from the moment the starting whistles blows right through to the end of the game.

Left and right midfielders are integral to the success of a soccer team.

Not only will you play an important role in moving the ball between the outer thirds of the field, but you will also be shoring up the defense and providing extra support for attacks.

This is a position where there is no room for blunders or mediocrity.

Learning to be the best wide midfielder you can be will provide your team with the extra support it needs to succeed.

Shooting with preceission and plan

Left and right midfielders often see more action than anyone else in the game. As a midfielder, you have a complex and diverse set of duties, along with a wide area to cover.

Although you have an important role in defense, you are also responsible for backing up the forwards and performing other offensive duties.

To confuse matters ever further, the number of right and left midfielders used in a game varies from team to team, and even from game to game.

Left and right midfielders are the true multitaskers in the game of soccer. At any given moment you could find yourself tackling, dribbling, passing, or shooting.

While these are all important skills for the role, many midfielders have the most trouble with shooting, especially with regards to when to shoot and where to shoot to.

During soccer games you can often see left and right midfielders taking shots that make no real sense to the game strategy.

Like all weaknesses, this shooting confusing can be made stronger with a little knowledge and subsequent action.

Below are a few questions and answers worth considering before attempting any long shots.

1. *What is the actual chance of the shot being successful?*
   If you are taking a long shot with only a small window of opportunity, then you are already at a huge disadvantage. Add to that the many variables that can mess with any shot at a goal, and you have a low potential for scoring and a high potential for missing or interception from the opponents.

2. *How heavily are you guarded?* If you are surrounded with opposing players, your best bet may be to pass the ball to a nearby teammate or to dribble out of the danger zone before even considering a shot at the goal.

3. *Does the shot stand a better chance if made by another player or from another angle?* Quite often, what seems like an impossible shot from a left or right midfielder's perspective, is actually quite achievable when passed over to a forward.

4. *What is the likely outcome if the shot fails?* This is very important to consider. If a failed shot delivers the ball back to the opposition, then the game can change in an instant, usually to the benefit of the rival side.

5. *What is your history of success with similar type shots in the past?* The chances are that you have taken similar shots either in other games or in practice sessions. The outcome of those shots is a good indicator as to whether the current attempt will be a success or not, depending on your previous attempts. Simply make your decision based on the above.

This may sound like a lot of decision making for the few nanoseconds you have prior to taking a shot, but once you become mindful of these things you will be able to run them through your mind in no time at all.

Don't forget too, that it takes a lot longer to read something than it does to think it, so try not to be put off by the details.

Just remember that by taking a shot on hope alone is simply foolhardy and can leave your team at a profound disadvantage.

Putting a little thought into the timing and odds of every potential shot can make a huge difference in the quality of your game.

The more you do this, the quicker you'll be able to process your decision making.

Accelerating in right situations

Left and right midfielders are constantly on the move. Back and forth across the field they go, backing up forwards, and shoring up defense. These players are often just a blur to spectators.

If you are a left or right midfielder, then you probably leave every game totally exhausted. Conserving energy, whenever possible, can be very important in this position.

There best way left and right midfielders can save energy is by knowing when to accelerate and when to not.

Sometimes, it's all too easy to just race after the ball and get caught up in the moment, but that doesn't mean it's always necessary.

Conserving energy is something that every soccer player talks about and agrees with, but it's not always something they're very good at following through on, especially once a high-tempo game kicks off and adrenaline gets released into the bloodstream.

Seriously, there are times when almost every player could conserve his energy more efficiently, and that is something that can only result in real benefits for his performance.

Below are a few situations that will help you to decide when it's best to accelerate, and when to stay back and conserve valuable energy.

Accelerate when:

- You must rush to get to the ball before an opponent. This is truly an emergency situation and the exact type of occasion that you are supposed to be saving your energy for.

- Accelerate when: A teammate needs your back up immediately. Support is one of your key duties so you can't neglect it.

- Accelerate when: You have an opportunity to get away from a player who is marking you. This will leave you open and therefore better positioned to help in a play or for an attempted shot at the goal.

- Accelerate when: You have the ball and an opponent is moving in. This is particularly necessary when there are no viable passing options.

- Accelerate when: Moving quickly will result in a score for your team, or prevent a score for the opposing side.

- Accelerate when: Moving off in a certain direction will "fake out" opponents and lead them away from your team's next strategic move. This can be a great strategy when your team just needs a few seconds of distraction to get better composed.

- Accelerate when: An opponent is on your tail. If quick acceleration is the only way to elude him, then by all means go for it.
- Accelerate when: You have just completed one strategic move and need to move quickly to your next position so that you can keep with the flow of the game.

Do not accelerate when:
- Another teammate is closer and more capable of handling the situation without your assistance. There's no need for you to wear yourself out if someone else is there and ready to perform the task at hand.
- Do not accelerate when: There is another left or right midfielder in the area that you were thinking of accelerating toward. Left and right midfielders can play interchangeably. Let the closer one handle the situation if he is in a position to do so.
- Do not accelerate when: Speed won't change the outcome of the play you have planned. Do not waste your energy by rushing around when it won't affect the end result.

Have you ever reached the latter stages of a game and found that your performance was deteriorating fast due to sheer muscle exhaustion and general fatigue?

Knowing when and when not to accelerate, and then using this knowledge wisely during games, will make the world of difference to your energy levels throughout the entire competition.

Players often don't realize just how many short bursts of unnecessary sprinting they perform during a game, but these all add up, and they eventually sap you of those much needed energy reserves. Well, they don't have to anymore.

There is nothing lazy or selfish about reserving energy for when it's most needed. In fact, it's the smart way to play.

You are simply investing your power into the right plays, for areas of your game where it is certain to pay off.

This is an approach that's good for you and good for your team.

One way passing alternatives

It's easy to fall into the trap of one-way passing.

This is where one player takes possession of the ball and then passes it to another player, who then hopefully scores.

Sounds perfect and logical, right? So you might be then wondering why it's a potential trap.

Well, the reason this style of play is potentially dangerous is because it creates a very predictable pattern.

It might be easy and comfortable for players to execute, but the downside is that it's equally as easy for the opposing team to figure out your style.

Once they do this, they can then effortlessly intercept your game because of your obvious performance.

So while one-way passing is an easy rut to fall into, it is still a rut nonetheless, and should therefore be avoided. For a left or right midfielder, it is particularly easy to fall into this trap.

Because this position includes both offensive and defensive capabilities, a left or right midfielder is uniquely suited to be the first party in a one way pass, meaning he's the passer.

And because he tends to stay on the flanks of the game, the one-way pass also helps him to avoid awkward diagonal shots and therefore remain in his position from where he's obviously most comfortable.

On the face of things, the one-way pass is perfect, but don't be fooled into using it during competitions.

So as you can see, the one-way pass becomes the easier, more natural option available, even though it's actually the worst possible choice you can make for the predictability reasons mentioned earlier.

Let's now take a look at what you can do, or more specifically, what you should be doing, instead of the much maligned one-way passes.

These alternatives are also easy, though much more effective and fun to execute once mastered.

- *Move forward on the field by passing the ball back and forth to each other.* This not only involves both players intimately in the game strategy, but it also reduces the risk of being tackled and losing the ball to an overzealous defensive opponent.

- *Give other players a chance*: A common problem with the one-way pass is that it often involves the same two people. This is not what you might call good teamwork. There are more than two players on the field, so be sure to pass the ball to the person who is in the best position to receive it, and not just to the person you favor (favoritism between friends is another trap to watch out for).
- *Develop plays that involve three or more different players*: Including more players in your game is a strategy that raises morale by promoting better teamwork. It also helps you to break out of your comfort zone (something else that is essential for personal development). Planning strategies that sometimes involve more than two people will help you to create a better framework for success.
- *Dribble*: Common soccer wisdom dictates that players should never dribble when they can pass instead. However, if you find yourself stuck in the one-way passing habit, then it's time to revisit those older skills to help steer your game in a new direction. The only way to break a bad habit is to replace it with something better, either as a stopgap or a permanent alternative.

- *Go for the score*: Don't pass the ball to a player so that they can shoot in situations where you are in a better position to take the shot yourself. Not only will the goalie be thrown off guard by your spontaneous actions, but the other team won't have as much opportunity to intercept the ball. More scores for less risk is a situation we can all live with.

The key to all of these techniques is confidence. Almost any play can be successful if it is executed with confidence and good form.

Learning new things from scratch can be a little daunting at times, but just know that all newly learned skills will build up your overall game repertoire and help you to become a much better player as a result.

Although it's easy for players in various positions to fall into the one-way passing habit, it is especially easy for left and right midfielders to get into rut.

If this is you, then it's time to break the bad habit and move your game up to a new level.

Defense – the other side of left and right midfielders

While playing a forward game is rewarding and gets you all the positive attention you could possibly ask for, backing up the defense is just as important in the grand scheme things. After all, one team's offense is another team's defense.

The exact kind of defensive skills that are required to perform the magic, versatility, and speed of left and right midfielders, is indeed a long and varied list.

Below are just a few of the most important defensive plays. These are the ones which are must-have requirements for anyone playing an effective game as a left or right midfielder.

1. *Intercepting wide passes and crossing them on the ground to a free player*. This move takes a ball that was posing a risk to your team and hands it to the forwards who can then use it to attempt a score. This is a defensive and offensive strategy in one easy play. Done well, it can singlehandedly turn a game around.

2. *Providing a strong presence on the flanks of the field*: This helps the defense by closing up any holes that could be exploited by the opposing team's forwards.

3. *Marking the opposition's left and right midfielders and wingers*. As talented and as capable as you might be, the other team probably has players of roughly the same caliber. Use your skills wisely to mark an equally talented opponent in an attempt to render him completely useless to his side. Your team will thank you later.

4. *Backing up defensive players however and whenever they need the assistance*: Every team has moments when they could use another pair of feet, and you can provide those feet if you are watching the defense closely for signs of distress. Left and right midfielders tend to be intuitive players, and backing up defensive players is one area where that intuition comes into its own.

5. *Making tackles on the opposing team's offense when the opportunity presents itself*: This is a common defensive job that is used by almost every player. Because players who are trying to break out often go wide, you will need to execute good tackling skills on a regular basis. Being well practiced in this skill will pay off with increased scores and high player morale.

Not only are players in this position known for their technical skills, but they are also known for their intelligence and intuition as well.

If you can handle balancing the needs of defense along with offensive duties, then you have what it takes to be a left or right midfielder.

If you are unsure, then the only way to find out is to give the position a try when the opportunity arises.

After playing a few games in this multi-tasking type role, you will either find that the duties become second nature to you, in which case you can then go on to develop still further, or the duties prove too much to handle, or at that particular time at least.

If the latter, then this position may not be your forte or perhaps you need to reconsider it again at a later date, once you have had time to further develop the skills necessary for the role.

Dueling as a left/right midfielder

Statistics have shown time and again that teams who win the most one-to-one duels are usually the teams that go on to win the games.

This puts a huge amount of pressure on left and right midfielders as they are the ones who face these kinds of duels in every game.

If you are a wide midfielder, learning how to win duels can have a huge effect on both your personal success and the success of your team.

Below are a few tips that will help you master the art of one-to-one dueling.

-   *Master your first-touch*: If you have to spend time getting the ball under control, then that will put you at a huge disadvantage. When opponents are moving in, you need to be able to get away quickly, so first touch soccer is your only option in situations where time is of the essence.

- *Face attacks head on:* Whether you are the player with the ball or the player trying to take the ball, you should approach the duel head on. Although players often try to dribble around opponents, this approach often leads into traps. Going straight forward, on the other hand, can intimidate opponents to the point where they simply get out of your way, thus preventing the duel from happening altogether. If you are trying to take the ball, facing your opponent will often cause them to try and go around you. If you continue to move so that you are always in front of them, they will often become flustered. This is the time when it becomes easiest to retake possession of the ball.
- *Learn to fake:* One of the most popular fakes involves stepping over the ball, and then turning toward it sharply before then moving away. If this particular move doesn't work for you, then make sure you find another fake that does. Faking moves convincingly allows you to lose opponents altogether or at least throw them off long enough to put some distance between the two of you.
- *Practice changing direction quickly, both with and without the ball:* This will allow you greater speed and give you a distinct advantage over less agile players. Become a master of this skill and you will be able to disorient opponents enough to win almost every duel.

- *Work on changing pace while maintaining good control of the ball*: If you cannot lose a fast-approaching opponent, slowing down abruptly will cause them to run right past you. Likewise, being able to pick up the pace quickly will allow you to leave them in the dust.
- *Improve your endurance*: The player who tires first is almost always the player who loses the ball. By working constantly on improving and maintaining both your stamina and your ability to put out spontaneous bursts of speed, you will be able to outlast and outperform the other players.
- *Don't get flustered*: Allowing emotions to overcome you will only cloud your thinking and allow opponents to win the duel. If someone is trying to upset or intimidate you, don't give them the satisfaction of complying. A calm head is a clear head and a clear head aids better performance.
- *Practice dueling*: Although this seems obvious, nothing will add to your dueling success as much as performing duels over and over. Every practice session for a left or right midfielder should involve lots of dueling. This will allow you to acknowledge your strengths and identify any weaknesses more clearly. Practicing duels in between competitions will also help to make you more comfortable going up against formidable opponents during real games.

Building the skills needed to excel at one-to-one duels is hard work, but it is work that will pay off big time, especially for left and right midfielders.

Wingers (LW/RW) - The Special Ones

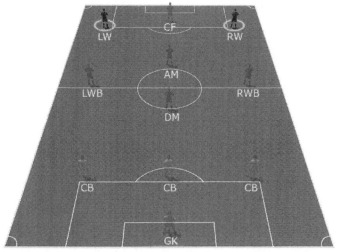

Many soccer players start out by wanting to become wingers, yet not so many succeed in the position. It takes a strong, skilled and incredibly determined player to step into these cleats.

To begin with, wingers need to be able to run up and down the field without needing to stop and catch their breath every two minutes.

They also need to be able to move the ball quickly, either by running with it, dribbling, or crossing.

Before applying for the position of winger on your team, there are a few important things you will need to consider first.

What is a winger, exactly?

Wingers are very special players because they play both defensive and offensive roles. They can be found on the edge of the field – in the wings (see illustration above).

As a winger, a typical game will include moving the ball, crossing to other players, and even moving in to the goal area.

As you can see, this is a demanding role that requires a multitasker with good ball handling skills and plenty of energy.

Essential skills

As a winger you will be playing in defensive, offensive and even midfielder capacities.

Therefore, you will need to possess a well-rounded set of skills. You will also need to be able to cross the ball with great power and accuracy.

Ball handling skills such as the ability to perform "stop and go" moves are also important.

Positional awareness is another crucial talent for the winger positions. This is because you play close to the boundaries.

Strength is not quite as vital to this position compared to others on the field like fullback or the defensive midfielder, but good speed and endurance are absolutely essential.

Speed and endurance are without doubt the two most important traits you need to have as a winger.

The reason for this is because you have to beat the opponents and then deliver the ball to your forwards while opponents languish in the dust of you fast actions.

Essential personality traits

Unlike many other soccer positions, the best wingers are not actually that aggressive.

Although they can and often do score goals, they are equally relegated to a role supporting the offense. This makes teamwork an essential ability for wingers.

Versatility and the ability to change direction quickly, both mentally and physically, are yet more important traits.

Discipline is another, something that comes in very handy on the field. Although wingers have a wide range of space, this can be a burden to them at times because it becomes all too easy to wander.

Having good discipline keeps you focused and helps you stay in the game, where you are most needed.

As a winger you will need to practice harder and more often than most of your teammates as you need more endurance and a wider range of skills overall.

Benefits and drawbacks

The main benefit of being a winger is that the role comes with a diverse range of duties.

If you are someone who is easily bored, then this is a position that will definitely keep you busy every moment of the game.

If you often find that you have problems mustering up the aggressive attitude that other positions require, then you may enjoy being a winger.

However, if you are someone who needs to bask in the limelight, then this is definitely not the right position for you, which brings us on to that very point.

Is the position of winger right for you?

Whether the position of winger is right for you or not depends on your skill set and your needs as a player. If you have great ball skills and are fast on your feet, then you have a good head start.

If you are comfortable with attention yet happy to let others take most the glory, you have the perfect personality for this position.

Although wingers definitely have their place in the sun, most of the time they play a supportive role on the team.

As a winger, you will find that you are always busy and often overwhelmed. This is not a position where you will spend much time waiting for the ball.

If you have the speed and stamina to move the ball up and down the field, good goal scoring capabilities, and the best cross on your team, then this position is absolutely perfect for you.

While all of these abilities can be developed, having natural talent in some of these areas will definitely give you an advantage.

The list of necessary traits for the winger position is so long and diverse that few people meet all the requirements from the outset, meaning this is not a job that anyone can just step into without having to develop in some areas at least.

Still, practice is not something that any soccer player shies away from if he's serious about playing in the position he has set his heart on.

If you fit the bill and are dedicated to the game and ready to put in the hours of practice necessary, then you too can become the team's star winger if you set your heart on it.

Your tactical responsibilities

If you are confused about your tactical responsibilities as a winger, you are alone. This is one position where things are not as clear cut as they perhaps should be.

While this is a multi-talented, multitasking position, it is so diverse in nature that beginners, and even intermediate players, just don't know exactly where their primary responsibilities lie half the time.

Below are a few pointers that will help to better define the job description of a winger:

- *He makes forward runs*. Because these can be very tiring, limit these to when there is no other alternative. When used effectively and conservatively, this move has the effect of a shock and awe attack, that is, it's completely unexpected and makes the opponents stop in their tracks for a moment, wondering what just happened.
- *He stays on the outside whenever possible*: This provides you with a unique vantage point from where to analyze the field, giving you visibility when it matters the most. Wingers are supposed to work the wings of the game, hence their name.
- *He moves the ball forward*: Moving the ball forward takes it ever closer to goal, which is exactly where you want it to be. Even if you don't make a goal yourself, another teammate will likely get a shot, thanks to your efforts.
- *He marks opponents*: Effectively marking opponents will help to keep them out of the defense's way. If you are on the wings, where you belong, this also keeps opponents out of the game play.
- *He creates and maintains width in your team's attack*: This prevents holes where opponents can break away and potentially score. It also forces the opposing team to divide, which is how they are best conquered.

- *He creates space for teammates*: If your teammate has got control of the ball and is planning to make a run for it, you can help greatly by keeping the opposition back and out of the way. Creating space can make all the difference in whether a play like this is successful or not.
- *He beats the opposition's fullbacks*: These guys are playing in the same area as you, so watch out for them. You will need to consistently be the faster, more alert, and more skilled player if you're to beat the opposition's fullbacks.
- *He delivers crosses to the strikers, who are usually in or near the penalty box*: This allows the strikers to take shots and hopefully score goals.
- *He scores, whenever possible*: There is no need to pass the ball to a teammate if you yourself have an open opportunity to score with your next move. Always take advantage of holes in the defense whenever and wherever you find them.

As you can probably tell by now, your job as a winger is not to just perform a wide range of jobs, but to perform them with speed, accuracy, and stealth.

You will need to be a bit crafty as a winger too, and be constantly thinking ahead in order to take full advantage of the versatility of this position.

Wingers really do perform a valuable and irreplaceable role in the game of soccer, especially in the complex and competitive atmosphere of modern games.

Building endurance for wingers

For many soccer players, the most challenging part of any game is the huge output of energy required over a relatively long time frame.

While every dedicated soccer player leaves the field exhausted, no players feel this demand quite as much as the wingers.

Although wingers are stationed on the wings of the field, they must still move up and down the field constantly throughout a game, as situations demand. This requires an enormous amount of endurance.

In fact, many players who have all of the skills necessary to be a winger find themselves unable to perform well in this position due to the excessive demand on energy.

If you want to be a winger but feel that you need to build up your stamina first, see below for some suggestions that will help you to work effectively on this area.

- *Before beginning any program, set some goals:* Perhaps you want to be able to run two miles without stopping, or sprint a certain distance in a set time? Regardless of the goals you pick, the most important thing is that you do choose goals and you write them down. Once set down in black and white, you then work tirelessly until you accomplish whatever the objective is. Many people find that planning a reward for when they have met their goal gives them a good incentive to push harder toward it.

- *Run several times a week*: Soccer players, on average, run five to six miles in every game, but wingers far exceed this. If you can run this distance easily, you are bound to perform better than a player who isn't in such good condition. The only way to build up your ability to run long distances is to run on a regular basis. However, don't focus only on racing at a sprinter's pace. Vary your pace between bursts of fast running and longer stretches, at a more reasonable jog, just as you would do during an average soccer game.
- *Jump rope at least once a week*: Most soccer players do not stay on the ground at all times, and wingers are no exception. Because jumping requires different muscles than running and kicking, you will improve your endurance immensely by regularly working these other muscle groups using a jumping rope.
- *Practice changing speed and direction*: Changing speed and direction ensures that you work other muscle groups, but equally as important is that this type of exercise will imitate the way you move in actual games. Because soccer does not involve running on a paved track, in a single direction, and at a constant speed, neither should your endurance training. Changing directions, turning, running at angles, running backward, and running at a variety of speeds will all mimic the pattern of a typical game, and therefore give you a distinct advantage over players who aren't practicing these skills.

- *Work your body until your muscles cannot take any more exertion:* Pushing yourself until your muscles can do no more is the fastest and most effective way to build endurance and improve overall strength. However, it's also important to know your limits and not try and push beyond them.
- *Take a day off after strenuous training sessions:* This is especially important if you are working to the point of extreme fatigue as suggested above. Overtraining is a serious issue for amateurs and professionals alike. Too much too often is a surefire way to permanently damage your body and cut your career short by years. Although it's important to push yourself, balance this by allowing ample recovery time.

The bad news is that soccer is one of the most physically demanding sports in the world. However, this is only really bad news if you aren't in peak physical condition.

The good news is that there are concrete steps you can take to develop your endurance and improve your success as a winger.

So with a little dedication and a lot of hard work, you can train your body and build up the stamina levels required to outlast and outrun the competing opponents.

Learning to play with both feet

Learning how to play soccer with both feet is a challenge for every player, but it is crucial if you're to take your game up to the next level.

Being able to use both feet, and use them equally well, gives any player twice as many chances to pass, shoot, and score than he would otherwise get with just a one-footed approach.

The two-foot skill reduces the amount of time spent shifting from foot to foot, thus making a player faster as well as more versatile. Nowhere on the field is the advantage of playing with both feet as beneficial as it is for wingers.

Because one of a winger's key duties is to move the ball to forwards and strikers with precise, well-timed passes, they can double their value on the team just by learning to use both feet effectively.

Many players balk at using their non-prominent foot because of the difficulty in mastering the skill.

Those who stick with it, on the other hand, often find that it's easier than they first thought, especially after they have gotten over the initial awkwardness.

Some players will become really proficient at using both feet, whereas others will be less so.

Be that as it may, all those who at least try will definitely become better at playing with both feet than they were before they worked on the skill.

When you perform various drills during practice sessions, give equal time to both feet whenever you can. This will prove awkward at first, to say the least, but don't let a little awkwardness put you off.

Switching from foot to foot regularly will eventually become second nature to you, or certainly much less uncomfortable than when you first started working on the skill.

One of my personal favorites for getting the non-prominent foot working is to juggle the ball. Juggling forces you to use both feet quickly and effectively, or it will do once you've got used with it.

Juggling is a great way to build up basic skills in general, but it's especially good for getting both feet working.

You might also try kicking a ball against the wall with your non-prominent foot.

This works best if you mark a place on the wall and aim for that. What this approach does is let you work on accuracy as well as form at the same time.

During practice you should try to play on the opposite side of the field from time to time too.

This will force you to use your non-prominent foot for a variety of plays, including dribbling, crossing, and passing.

By trading positions with another winger you both get to gain valuable experience and improve your abilities in this area.

As you get better at using both feet, you can begin to confidently alternate the sides which you approach opposing players.

Not only will this force you to use both feet in in your game, it may also throw off your opponents by forcing them to play with their weaker foot.

Practicing with your non-prominent foot will prove difficult at first. Still, just stick with the plan and never lose focus on the benefits it will reward you with once you become comfortable using either of your feet.

The moment you are able to play equally with both feet, or as near to equal as you can get, you will increase your chances of succeeding exponentially in all kinds of different situations.

Good timing and awareness for runs

If you are already a winger in soccer, you probably spend a lot of your time making runs.

Although this is an important part of a winger's job, there are many good reasons to use good timing and awareness when making these runs.

Below are a few instances that look at both the right times and the wrong times to make runs:

Right times to make a run:
- When it is the most effective or only safe way to exchange a ball. Sometimes a cross or other pass simply isn't going to work. In this situation, a run is a necessary and logical choice.
- Right time to make a run: When it distracts your opponent. Sometimes you may not be able to make it to a teammate to help them out, yet making a run will attract your opponent's attention enough to give your teammate a greater chance of success.

- Right time to make a run: When running forces your opponent to commit to a move. This will allow you to be more proactive in your game.
- Right time to make a run: When you are temporarily exchanging positions with a teammate. This is often done to confuse opponents and create opportunities for your own team. As long as you make sure all positions are covered and you return to your position after the play is complete, this is a solid strategy that is definitely worth your time and energy.
- Right time to make a run: When you can stay wide. This allows you to stay in position while at the same time allowing room for various plays.
- Right time to make a run: When you can disguise the run so that the other team is caught off guard. If making a run allows you to get into position for another play, while at the same time staying under the radar, it can be a good strategic choice.
- Right time to make a run: When you have a good idea of what chain of events will follow your run. In soccer, as in most life situations, having a plan or end goal improves your chances of success. If you have a plan that begins with you making a run, go for it. However, don't be afraid to change your plan at the last minute if the situation calls for it.

Wrong times to make a run:

- When making the run takes you far away from the place you will be needed shortly. Obviously you cannot teleport around the field, so staying in position during an important play makes good sense.

- Stay put: When making the run opens up a hole in the soccer field that opponents could exploit to their advantage. Even if your run 'might' have a good result, it's rarely worth giving your opponents an opportunity to get an upper hand, especially since that upper hand may lead to a score for their side.

- Stay put: When the opposing team is expecting your run and prepared to deal with it. This is something that you don't know as much as you have a hunch for. Either way, don't set yourself up for failure by taking the obvious and expected route.

- Stay put: When passing will produce the same result. Although this seems obvious, it is not unusual to see wingers eager to run about the field when there are easier, quicker options. Show good common sense and be a selfless player, one who allows others to take the ball and the spotlight too.

While there is no way to list all the different situations you will encounter in a soccer game, what's most important is that you evaluate each situation separately to determine whether making a run or staying put is the better option.

As a winger, clear thinking, good timing, and an awareness of the game overall, are as important as any other skill and should be worked on as such.

The more you are mindful of your situations, the quicker you will become at using your better judgments for deciding whether to run or not.

Learn to avoid offside calls

Although most soccer rules are straightforward enough, the offside rule is frequently misunderstood by avid fans and experienced players alike.

Not only do the offside rules vary in different circumstances, but misunderstanding them can carry some pretty harsh consequences, things like giving your opponents a free indirect kick or giving up a hard-won goal.

Wingers are especially prone to offside calls. The main reason for this is because they regularly move on the offensive without the ball in their possession.

This is something that can be misinterpreted by a referee as being distracting to opposing players.

However, with a little knowledge, there is no need for your team to suffer another offside call.

The offside rule can be frustrating and carry a high cost for your team when broken, but it is also easy enough to avoid if you and your teammates follow a few basic guidelines.

Below are a few instances that, when heeded, will result in you never be called offside again.

- You are never offside when you are on your own team's side of the soccer field. This is the most basic part of the offside rule.
- You cannot be offside unless you are in active play, whether moving the ball, moving into position for a play, or somehow interfering with other players.
- You will never be called offside when there are two opposing players on the defense between you and the ball, even if one of these players is the goalie.
- You will never be called offside if you are either behind or with the soccer ball, or behind or with a defender, other than the goalie.
- You will never be called offside if you are the recipient of a corner kick. However, once you have passed the ball on, you are once again subject to the offside rule.

Knowing when you are you offside can be complicated at times.

This is because several factors must occur simultaneously in order for this to happen.

Below are a few of the most common instances when offside calls are made.

- You are offside when you are positioned between the goal and the ball with only the goalie (or other defensive opponent) nearer to the goal than you.
- You can be offside when you are playing the ball, about to play the ball, distracting an opponent, blocking an opponent, or otherwise in active play. This can include a variety of activities, including distracting a goalie or moving into a formation.
- You can be offside even if you are accidentally in active play, for example, you accidentally block a defensive player. It's best to always stay in a formation where you can never be misinterpreted.

The only way to prevent the other team from getting those valuable free indirect kicks is to memorize these rules and keep them in the forefront of your mind at all times.

Note that any goals made while you are offside will not be counted.

Honestly, there is no worse feeling than having a score disallowed because you have been called offside.

Not fully understanding the offside rule carries a high price, not only for you but also for your team. Breaking this rule can literally affect the outcome of a game.

Many soccer fans and players question the reasoning behind the offside rule, not least because it seems both unnecessarily complicated and rather pointless most of the time.

However, despite people's gripes, there are actually very good reasons for the offside rule, just as there are for all other soccer rules and regulations that apply to the game.

Offside rules force soccer players to play in teams and to move as a line with the ball. If this rule wasn't in place you might see one or two people running around in a ragtag fashion doing their own thing, and that style of play just isn't soccer.

So by having the offside rule, teams are forced to play a better game of soccer, the way it's supposed to be played.

Furthermore, by adhering to these rules, fans have more maneuvering to watch on the field, thus providing the kind of entertainment the game was invented for.

In brief, soccer is a team sport, and the offside rule ensures that the game is always played as it was intended; as two teams competing against each other, as two teams, and not 22 individuals running around a field doing their own thing.

Forward Line Is All About Scoring

Although forward line players have the narrowest range of skills, it is still important that they are able to perform well in various situations, and sometimes that means more than just shooting at the goalmouth.

Their primary duty is to score goals, first and foremost, but any shortcomings on their part will obviously have an impact on the team's statistics.

If you are hoping to become a forward line player then take a look at the useful list of skills below.

These are what every attacker needs to master if he's to become successful in the position.

Learning these skills will help to build confidence and therefore performance levels in all the right areas.

- *Passing with accuracy*: Passing is an essential skill for the forward line because it can distract opponents enough to open up new scoring opportunities. Just because you are unable to score at a precise moment in time, that doesn't mean another teammate can't. There are several ways to practice your passing, but the most common and most effective is also the most straightforward. Work at your passing skills simply by kicking the ball back and forth with a teammate. There are also several passing drills that you can use to overcome any flaws in your form.

- *Receiving without making mistakes*: In general, for every pass you make you will receive the ball equally as often. Receiving the ball with accuracy, as well as an effective first touch, is one of the most important skills for a forward line player. Because most passing drills also involve receiving the ball, this makes them an effective means of practice. Another way to develop receiving skills is to place a piece of paper on a wall, or some other marker, and then practice by kicking the ball at the paper, receiving it, and immediately kicking it back. This is effective because you will not just be receiving, but receiving from a variety of angles, and then immediately returning the ball with a high level of accuracy. As a bonus, this practice does not require another player, so you can perform it almost anywhere where there's a wall at your disposal.

- *Dribbling without fear*: In a situation crowded with opponents, shooting and passing will not always be possible. At times like these, dribbling is usually the only option. Dribbling with skill and accuracy will allow you to move away from bad situations quickly, and hopefully create other scoring opportunities for you and other players in the process. Most forward line players benefit from basic dribbling drills that involve moving around obstacles, such as dribbling around different configurations of cones or dribbling through fields of strategically placed teammates, as two examples.
- *Creating scoring opportunities*: No forward line player, however talented, can singlehandedly score all the goals for his team. If you want to be successful on the forward line, you must share both the responsibility and the glory with others. A good rule of thumb is that you should create twice as many scoring opportunities as you take personally. Although there are no drills that effectively teach this skill, you can become a better team player by consciously giving opportunities to your teammates in every game, obviously only when it's the best option at the time. It can be tempting to take every shot whenever the ball lands at your feet, but the best players will know if the chance of scoring is more likely if the ball is passed over to another, better positioned player at any given moment.

- *Heading with power:* Because you will have to receive airborne balls and turn them into goals from time to time is why heading is another essential skill for forward line players. Not only will you need to head the ball with correct form, but you will also need to head it with precision too. One good practice drill for this involves two other teammates. One of the teammates tosses the ball to you which you then head to the other teammate. The faster you can perform this action with accuracy, the better you will become at headings when playing in competitions.
- *Shooting with accuracy:* Shooting is your primary responsibility as a forward line player. If you are bored with your normal repertoire of shooting drills, here is one that might inspire new enthusiasm. For this you will need to involve several players who will form two lines facing each other from some distance. Spread the players out within their respective lines so that they are 4-5 feet apart (they should be able to spread their arms out from the sides without touching each other). Give a ball to one side and have the first player shoot it at the other line. Someone on the other side will likely intercept it. The player who received the ball can then shoot it back. Going back and forth like this is fun and helps players to develop their shooting accuracy. If you are used to shooting with five or more players defending the goal, then a normal game situation will seem easy in comparison to this drill.

Centre Forward (CF) - The Tank

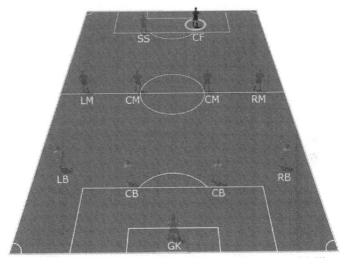

Many soccer players like to, or at least would like to, play the position of centre forward, and it's easy to see why.

The centre forward is one of the players most likely to score goals. He is therefore one who gets to bask in all the recognition and applause that comes with scoring.

Centre forwards are not just standing around waiting for someone to serve them the ball.

These players, like others on the team, are hard workers too, even though they are recipients of the hard work done by the defensive and midfield players.

But centre forwards must also be skilled, capable and mentally strong if they are to be successful in their role.

What is a centre forward?

A centre forward is responsible for scoring many of the team's goals. These players tend to be central to the team's most crucial moves and are therefore very visible.

This is the position that everyone wants to play, yet few people get the chance because they simply don't have what it takes to excel.

Centre forwards tend to be large and intimidating, but they are also agile at the same time. Being a good height is a real advantage in this position.

Essential skills

First and foremost, a centre forward must be able to score goals, and plenty of them. He must be competent at scoring from a variety of angles and in all kinds of different situations.

He needs to be able to do this while he's under close guard, and often taking his opponents completely by surprise.

The success of the entire team is dependent on the centre forward's ability to get that ball into the goal.

This requires that he has the kind of ball skills that can only come from a combination of raw talent and countless hours of diligent practice.

Controlling the ball is one of the most essential skills of a centre forward. No one will hand you the ball or clear a direct path to the goal in preparation for your shot.

You must be able to receive the ball, maneuver it, and keep it safe from the many opponents crowding around in your area.

Self-protective skills are another must-have capability. No player is as well guarded and as well watched by the opposition as the centre forward, so knowing how to elude defensive players is absolutely necessary.

Essential personality traits

Centre forwards need to be both brave and tough. They have to go up against some pretty intimidating defensive opponents at times, and they do get knocked around a fair bit as a consequence.

Being able to stay calm and not take rough treatment personally will help you deal with the jostling that comes with the position.

Good general instincts and intuition will help you immensely as a centre forward.

Centre forwards often play with their back to their opponents or to their own team. This requires a natural, intuitive ability to sense what is going on behind you before you get to look.

Benefits and drawbacks

The key benefit to playing centre forward is that you will be your team's star player, or one of the star players (most of the time).

While it is nice to get lots of credit for the team's victories, the key drawback is that you, as the centre forward, will also be held responsible, to some extent, for team losses too.

These players are usually judged solely by their number of scores. Although this can be unfair in many circumstances, it is something that comes with the territory nonetheless.

You just have to accept the accolades while letting criticism, fair or unjust, go in through one ear and out through the other.

While the centre forward can be the most celebrated player on the team, this praise is not something that is given to him freely.

This is a position that requires a lot of hard work and concentrated effort at all times.

Should you play as centre forward?

Many people think they have what it takes to play the position of a centre forward, but often find that the demands become too much for them to handle.

In other words, it's a much harder job than its description first depicts.

Having a go is the only surefire way to find out if you have the right blend of courage, toughness, tactical ability, and ball skills needed for the position.

Not all jobs on the soccer field suit all players, no matter how enthusiastic or talented they might be, but most of us find our niche, eventually.

The only way to find your forte is to try out for the various positions that interest you, and then see which one fits you the best.

Just as many try for the position of centre forward and decide soon afterward not to pursue it further, so have plenty of others found great success and happiness playing in this position, and you could be the next.

Five reasons not to chase every ball

As a centre forward it is tempting to go after every ball that comes your way.

Because you are the most offensive player, and the main scorer for the team, whenever a ball comes into sight it can be a potential goal, in your eyes at least.

No one wants to miss an opportunity to score. This is why many centre forwards are diligent about gaining and maintaining control over the ball the moment it enters their domain.

As a centre forward, you may prefer to stay in or near the penalty box at all times. This will mean that you are always ready and in place to take every opportunity to score.

Some centre forwards have superior technical skills and use their excellent ball control and perfect aim to score impressive goals.

Other centre forwards are known for scoring plenty of goals using their head.

And there are some who like to go and get the ball themselves, although these types are the players who tend to get winded and exhausted easily and therefore not as useful to the team as they could otherwise be.

However you play your game, just remember that conserving energy for when it's most needed is fundamental to your success.

That means there are times when you should not go after the ball, no matter how tempted you are to pursue it.

Below are the five main reasons why you should not chase every ball that comes your way:

1. *You'll wear yourself out*: Even players with a high level of stamina cannot chase the ball from one side of the field to the other for an entire game. If you want to be useful to your side from beginning to end, then you need to be wise when it comes to conserving your energy.

2. *You'll make yourself the center of attention*: While every player wants to be a star, drawing too much attention to yourself will make the other team take more notice of you. The result of this means you'll be better guarded by the opposing defense and better watched by the opposing goalie.

3. *The midfielders are there to pass the ball to you.* When you leave the penalty box to go after the ball, you may be stepping on toes, both literally and figuratively. The field is crowded with players, so letting a teammate receive the ball and then pass it over to you is usually the best practice.

4. *You'll be busy when the time comes for an easy score.* Imagine an opportunity to score materializes but when the winger goes to pass the ball to you you're not there. The winger can then take the shot himself, from a less advantageous angle, or the opportunity gets missed altogether. There's a good reason for your position in the formation of the team, and this is most evident when your absence causes a lost opportunity.

5. *The top centre forwards use different styles as necessary.* Stay near the penalty box when necessary, use various skills when the game demands it, head the ball if an aerial shot comes your way, and sometimes even chase the ball when it's absolutely required. Not only is this diverse and structured style of play more likely to get you a score, but it will also help you to stay energized throughout the entire game.

Being a diverse player not only makes you better-rounded and better-equipped to handle a variety of situations, it also makes it difficult for your opponents to predict and counteract your moves.

Mixing up your dribbling moves

Because the centre forward is one of the main scorers on the team, you can be certain that the other side will be watching him very closely indeed.

This is where being a well-rounded player comes into its own.

By using a variety of passing and dribbling techniques you make it all the more difficult for opponents to predict your moves and clear the ball away from your feet.

Since centre forwards spend a lot of their time dribbling, here are a few different techniques to add to your repertoire:

- *The fake kick*: Here you are tricking the opponent by faking a shot. When the opponent tries to block the shot, you simply accelerate away from the area and leave him in the dust. This is a really good way to lose an opponent who is marking you closely.
- *The 360*: Place your foot firmly on the ball and push it slightly forward. Now put your weight on the ball and spin yourself around, changing direction. You can then push the ball in front of you with your foot before embarking on the next star play.

- *The scissors dribble*: This is a move that (when performed at pace) can trick almost any opponent. To perform it well you start by dribbling the ball with your feet, then plant your foot on the outside edge of the ball and swing your other leg over it in an arc. This is called an inside to outside step-over. You can then take the ball in the opposite direction. This is a great way to change direction really quickly and fool the opponents who are guarding you.
- *The lunge*: In this classic soccer move, you use your body to convince the opponent you are going in one direction and then take off in another. To do this you jump sideways around the ball, then lean toward the direction you are faking, suggesting you are about to head off that way, and then cut the ball in your actual direction using your other foot.
- *The chop*: The chop begins when you are dribbling the ball forward with your dominant foot. You then hit the ball inwards with the opposite foot and at the same time pass your other foot over the ball. Still confused? Don't worry. There are plenty of YouTube video demonstrations if you could use a little visual help with this move.

- *Stop and go*: The point of this move is to get your opponent to change pace by slowing down, or stopping even, so that you can pass them quickly and with an element of surprise. You do this when you are dribbling in a straight line. You then stop the ball abruptly with your foot. Your opponent will then slow down or hesitate, and as he does, you take the ball forward at full speed.

Using a variety of moves, especially the "fakes," will make sure your opponents never know what you are going to do next.

This style of play helps to create a confused and demoralized opposition. As a centre forward, being unpredictable may be your single best strategy.

Aerial ability Vs speed

If you closely study some of the top centre forwards in the game, you will see that they all have physical advantages which allow them to compete effectively against the opposing team's defenders.

Note how some are tall and lanky, while others are more compact and fast on their feet. So why do so many centre forwards fall into one of these two build categories?

Why are both height and speed such advantages in this particular position? Why can't a player be both tall and fast?

Well, starting with the tall players, these guys obviously have an immense advantage as centre forwards, otherwise there wouldn't be so many of them playing in this particular position.

You see, most of the opposing team's centre backs must jump five or more inches just to come out even. The tall centre forward in this situation has an obvious lead, and therefore gets to win heading duels most of the time.

In games where there are several heading duels, the team with a very tall centre forward will have a clear advantage over the opposition.

There are other advantages to being a tall centre forward besides that of winning heading duels.

Lofty players can see above others' heads and evaluate more quickly what is going on in other parts of the field.

Having long legs is also an advantage as they give extra leverage, thus resulting in more powerful kicks. A tall player also comes across more intimidating, especially to players considerably shorter than him.

This invariably helps to back off some defenders a lot easier.

OK, so what about those great centre forwards who fall into the other category of compact and speedy.

Well, these players are among the fastest of any sport in the world, most being chosen for the job because they are able to run one hundred meters in under eleven seconds.

Having extreme speed like this also gives players a huge advantage when going up against opponents.

While they may not be able to win every heading duel, they will often beat a defender to the ball, and because of that height is less of an issue.

Speed has other advantages too. Centre forwards who are very fast cannot only beat opponents to the ball, but also move around the field at a remarkable pace, quick enough to confuse opponents and execute some very complicated plays in the process.

These things combined lead to increased shooting and scoring opportunities for the team with the fastest centre forwards, which in itself is a huge benefit.

So height and speed seem to be what determines the best centre forwards, and it's easy to see why. Yet both height and speed in an individual is something that's pretty hard to come by, or at least extremely tall and extremely fast is.

In general, a larger, longer body is less aerodynamic and therefore takes more time and effort to move around.

This doesn't mean that really tall players can't be fast, because they can, and speed can always be improved for anyone of any shape or size.

Although really tall players can become faster through practice, they will rarely be the "fastest" on the field simply because of their build.

Likewise, if you are a centre forward of the smaller and speedier type, then you cannot add to your height, but you can learn to jump higher, even though you will never be the highest jumper on the team.

Regardless of which advantages you bring as a centre forward, the most important thing is that you work diligently to improve your weaker areas and constantly increase and maintain your existing strengths.

The real tough guys in soccer

There was a time when soccer was a sport for only the toughest of the tough guys.

Players were used to being knocked around and jostled, in fact it was all par for the course back then, in a time when injuries were more common than scores.

Today's soccer is definitely a softer sport compared to how it was with past generations.

The twenty-first century game sees a more polite and friendly competitor and a general approach that is pretty much hands-off, at least for most of the time.

However, there are still a couple of positions that must retain the flinty stance of that bygone age, and the centre forward is perhaps the most old-fashioned of these tough-guy roles.

Below are just a few of the discouraging, intimidating, and even downright painful situations you will face as a centre forward.

- *Being knocked around by centre backs:* Not only will you be taking numerous body hits from these large and in-charge players, but you will often be taking them in the back, when you're least expecting it. This is so common that a lot of centre forwards walk off the field at the end of a game with multiple bruises and scrapes.
- *Getting kicked:* It's not unusual for centre backs to get kicked. This is purely because they are always in the thick of the action. The most common place they experience kicks is on the foot, but most players have been kicked in the head at least once. It's just the price one pays for relentlessly pursuing the ball wherever it happens to go.
- *Collisions:* Players in your area of the field are constantly accelerating and decelerating. Because of this, it is almost impossible to accurately predict where any given player is going to be in few seconds time. This leads to numerous collisions. Although most of these human crashes are easy to shrug off, others can lead to serious injuries because of the high speeds and force involved.

There are several ways to reduce your chances of being severely injured during a game.

First, and perhaps the most important of all, is to make sure you warm up properly before every game.

What warming up does is loosen your muscles and gives you better reflexes when performing physical movements.

Seriously, the importance of warming up as a way to prevent injury cannot be emphasized strongly enough.

Muscles that are supple are a lot more flexible and therefore less likely to get damaged whenever the body makes sudden and extreme movements, as in the case of a collision or other intense and unexpected movements.

Another way to reduce the risk of injury is to wear any protective gear that's allowed for your level of play.

Some centre forwards find that ankle taping helps prevent sprains and other such injuries.

Wearing only quality footwear will also help to prevent unnecessary injury.

Having poorly made or ill-fitting soccer boots can significantly increase to your chances of injury for obvious reasons.

Finally, make sure that appropriate first aid gear, such as ice packs and bandages, are always available and close by.

It's quite often the case that the faster first aid is applied, the less intense the injury will become.

Furthermore, the recovery time may be reduced when first aid is applied quickly to an injury, depending on the type and severity of the injury, or course.

Not all injury is preventable. In actual fact, some injury is inevitable, to a greater or lesser extent, and the more you play soccer the higher the potential for injury becomes.

But by taking preventive measures, you will definitely reduce the risks of getting hurt and injured by quite a bit.

When you do get injured, it's important to respond with immediate and appropriate action.

If you are bleeding or severely hurt, then you should leave the field immediately and get help from your coach or another person who is trained to deliver first aid.

After you are treated, do not go back to the game until it is safe for you and the other players. Heed the advice of your coach or any medical professional that's on standby.

If necessary, go to a doctor after the game to check that no permanent damage has occurred or that no further treatment is necessary.

Again, listen to the advice of those with more experience than you on injuries.

You might be feeling fine, but that doesn't necessarily mean you will be.

Although it's important to prevent injury whenever you can, don't allow the potential of injury to occupy your thoughts too much.

If you let the fear of getting hurt govern the way you play soccer, then you will end up missing opportunities and underperforming because of your overcautious behavior.

In order to be a happy and successful centre forward, you need to be prepared to take your knocks and make light of them as and when they occur.

So prevent injuries the best you can and treat any that happen, as soon as they happen, but always get back on the field the moment you are able.

Getting jostled and bruised is simply part of soccer, especially in the position of centre forward. If you really want to avoid as much bone-on-bone contact as possible when playing the game, then this is definitely not the right position, for you.

Striker (S) – The Goal Scoring Machine

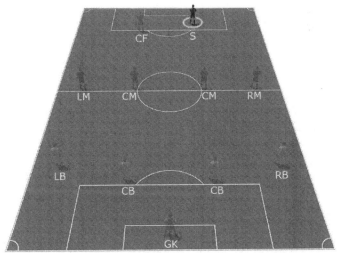

Although centre forwards get plenty of credit, the striker is usually the player who scores most goals overall.

Unlike the other team positions, the striker has only one sole duty, and that is to score as many goals as possible. That's it.

If you have good, single-minded concentration, and the ball handling skills necessary to make score after score, then the striker position might just be the perfect post for you.

Obviously not every player can meet the diverse requirements that this high-profile, high-pressured position calls for, but those who can get to relish in one of soccer's most celebrated jobs.

What is a striker?

A striker is an offensive player who simply scores goals.

That's it in a nutshell.

They play on the farthest end of the offensive third of the field.

Without them, winning a game would prove very difficult, if not impossible at times, because the other players are distracted by so many other duties.

Only scoring goals might sound like a simple duty but it is no easy feat.

A striker must deal with some very tough offensive players, and also have superior ball skills as well as a crafty knack of sneaking in a few surprises for the goalie.

Essential skills

A striker must be a goal-scoring machine, plain and simple. That means kicking with strength and accuracy is an absolute must have ability.

You, as a striker, will also need to be constantly aware of your position, and the position of the goal in relation to where you are at all times.

You must also have a clear understanding of the potential scoring opportunities that may derive from the many situations and angles of play.

Because scoring goals is a striker's only duty, he plays the game with a very high awareness of the goal area and the potential scoring chances as they materialize from moment to moment.

Good communication is an essential skill for any striker. He needs to direct the offensive players on his team to the positions where they can be supportive and/or protective of him.

He also needs to know how to read the cues of his fellow players.

This allows him to quickly take the ball when it comes his way and do something useful with it in a split second.

Being able to perform accurate and well-thought-out penalty kicks is also a good skill for strikers to possess.

Strikers are the obvious choice for penalty kicks and other well-placed kicks that can give the team an incredible advantage. Such skills can be easily learned in just a few practice sessions.

Essential personality traits

Having an ability to read people is a real asset in the position of striker.

You must be able to understand the goalie and other defensive players, and that means having the ability to identify their strategies and recognize any weak points among them.

Identifying and exploiting weak spots leads to more goals and more goals simply leads to more victories.

Assertiveness is another personality trait that will help you perform your duties with heightened success.

Whenever the defenders are guarding you closely, being assertive about your space will allow you to make the plays that will enable you to dominate in your domain.

If you impose enough presence on the field, then the opponents are more likely to get flustered and make mistakes, which can go on to open up even more opportunities for you and your side.

Benefits and drawbacks

The obvious benefit of this position is the wealth of recognition that comes with every goal and every win.

Along with the centre forward, you will be given a lot of credit for each and every victory.

However, the striker position is not without its negative side.

Because no team can ever win every single game, it means that there will be times where you have to take the blame for defeats too.

The blame game can often be an unfair one, but it is often the striker who takes most of the flak for any defeats.

This position can be an emotional roller coaster and can therefore prove too much to handle for a faint hearted or overly sensitive player.

Should you play as striker?

If you are fast, have good ball handling skills, and are a quick "forward thinking" player, then you have the potential to find great success in this position.

If you love the game of soccer with a passion, and really want to put yourself in the heart of the action, then this is the position that will fulfill all your needs.

This is not a position that suites everyone though, despite the fame and glory it promises for the right candidate.

For some individuals, the attention and pressure that a striker faces in every game is simply too much to bear.

Although most players dream of being a top striker, very few actually make the grade.

This is why soccer teams the world over are constantly searching for strikers with the right skills and the right temperament to succeed.

There is no player more valued than a good striker. He is the one who has the ability to decide the outcome of a game.

This is a position for players who want to be all-important and irreplaceable. It's also a position for players who can flourish under huge pressure, meaning they thrive under stressful situations, not crack.

If you think you have what it takes to fit into the boots of a striker, then it's time for you to get out on the field and give it a try.

If you're still on the fence, then keep reading as more specifics of the role are revealed.

Finish at the goal on the first touch

Soccer is a game of limited opportunities to actually play the ball. Even high action positions such as striker, often only have possession of the ball a few times in every game.

Because of this limited time with the ball, it is crucially important to take advantage of each and every opportunity to score a goal. From the moment the ball touches your feet, you should be looking for a chance to shoot and score.

By far the best way to increase the number of goals you score is by shooting more.

By making shooting the first option to consider every time the ball comes your way will get you into scoring mode, a state of mind where little else matters other than making goals.

Below are a few ways to optimize that first touch so that your attempts lead to more goals more often:

- *Know your space*: Knowing your space simply means being aware of your area on the field as the ball approaches you. Be ever mindful of where your opponents are at any given time, and this goes for your teammates too. After quickly assessing your surroundings you should be able to know in a second what direction to take the ball to maximize your chances of success. Quick thinking, not overthinking, is the only way to increase your chances of scoring goals the moment opportunities present themselves.

- *Receive the ball with your downfield foot*: The reason for this is because that is the foot which is closest to the goal you want to attack. Receiving in this way sets you up to score.

- *Take control immediately*: The only way to learn how to take immediate control of a ball, all of which will be approaching at various speeds, spins and angles, is to practice, over and over. Taking control of the ball is important because if you fail on the first attempt you will probably lose it and the opportunity to score.

- *Find your space*: No one can shoot at their best while being under immense pressure, so your next step should be to find a little unpressured space. While being quick is important, don't rush into an unsafe situation. Make sure you have the space to make a good shot. Even if the space you move into is only temporary, it only takes a few seconds to set up and make the shot that could save the game.
- *Don't be afraid to take risks*: If you are the hesitant type it means you are pausing for thought too much. Instead, try making quick moves without over thinking. Once you can do this several times successfully it will start to become second nature to you. You will then become more successful more often. This in turn will build your confidence and that means you will be more comfortable at taking risks.
- *Don't take stupid risks*: If you are the reckless type, take a moment to contemplate your shots. Ask yourself questions like: is there a better angle or another player better positioned to take the shot than you? Quite often, a missed shot is a shot that could have been successful under slightly different circumstances. Calculated risk taking is fine, whereas reckless risks can, and quite often do, lead to failure.

In the end, shooting is usually the better option compared to not shooting at all. Every moment that you have the ball is a moment it could be lost to the opposing team if you don't do something with it quickly.

That means there is very little time to do much else than to take a shot at the goal. Everyone knows the general rule that states you should always pass the ball before dribbling whenever there's a possibility. A good addendum to this rule is that you should always shoot before passing if the opportunity is there.

Scoring goals is a lot about confidence

Although physical and technical skills are central to the game of soccer, confidence also plays a huge part in both individual and team success.

Players in all positions need confidence to perform well, but it is perhaps the position of striker where confidence is most important.

A striker can practice his shooting techniques and enhance his technical ability as much as he wants, but without the confidence to fully utilize these skills in a game, well, such abilities are practically worthless.

That's how important self-confidence is to a player in this position. Indeed, many of the all-time great strikers such as Ronaldo Luís Nazário de Lima and Marco Van Basten, will tell you that confidence is absolutely fundamental to goal-scoring

Firing shots at the goal requires quick thinking, fast movements, and excellent judgment, all of which must be carried out under high pressure situations.

To facilitate good judgment a striker needs to be poised. He has to be sure of himself in the decisions he makes and the actions he takes.

Even the best players can suffer from a lack of confidence at times. When this happens, and for whatever reasons it happens, the only way out of the trap is for you to quickly build yourself back up before this lack of confidence takes a firm hold.

If you are looking to improve your goal-scoring confidence, here are a few useful tips that will definitely help you succeed.

1. *Use positive visualization when training, playing, or even just thinking about soccer. Always imagine your actions ending in a goal.* When you strike the ball, visualize exactly where and how it will hit the back of the net. Convince yourself that your task is an easy one, and that the opposing defenders and their goalkeeper will be mesmerized by your awesome shooting power and accuracy. This will help you follow through with your actions convincingly and deliberately.

2. *Be realistic. Understand that not all shots can be successful.* If you fail to score after firing a well-aimed missile at the goalmouth, don't let yourself get dragged down by it. Just dust yourself off quickly and move on with the game. In other words, forget about it. What's done is done and cannot be undone; it's as simple as that. Understand that dwelling on failed attempts means you are more likely to repeat the failure in future. All your attention should now be focused on the next opportunities you have to score. Keep going in a forward, positive direction and the goals will keep coming.

3. *Don't allow yourself to be intimidated by opposing team players:* Defenders and goalkeepers will sometimes try to knock your confidence by attempting dirty tricks; things aimed at getting under your skin and affecting your game. They might make negative comments as a way to distract you or lower your self-confidence. Some might even give you a sly kick to 'welcome you to the game.' If any of these things happen, try to take them as a compliment. Whatever you do, don't take the bait and bite back.

4. *Make sure your team maintains a positive and supporting atmosphere:* The support of your teammates is crucial for building confidence. By feeling comfortable in their midst you will be able to excel in your role on the team. Being spurred on and having good support behind you can do wonders for building and maintaining self-confidence. Remember to reciprocate this support too, by backing your teammates in much the same way that you like them to encourage you. If you criticize players, however, then they may take a negative attitude towards you as well, especially when any criticism is petty and uncalled for. Try to develop your own confidence in tandem with that of the team as a whole because they are both highly interrelated.

Remember that confidence is as important as any technical skill, and one simply can't succeed without the other.

A confident striker in a confident team will bag lots of goals and consequent success for the side. If you need more confidence, work on it, if you have it, maintain what you've got and you will go far in this game.

Vision, position and ambition

When most people think of the abilities that a striker needs to be successful, they generally think of certain ball skills such as shooting and passing as being the most important.

This position, in theory at least, is a relatively simple one. It generally boils down to braking through the opponent's defenses and scoring goals.

The best way a striker can break through his opponent's defenses is by having both good vision and positional awareness. This is easy to say, of course, but not quite so easy to carry out.

If you are having a hard time taking your striker career to the next level, then follow the step by step guide further down the page. This will help you to first understand and then develop your own good vision and positional awareness.

Having good vision can be defined as seeing patterns in the game and understanding how plays are developing, or likely to develop any moment soon.

Good vision allows you to see both goal-scoring opportunities and the moves that lead up to them. Quite often, a potential score is just a pass away. While vision can be somewhat tricky to learn, it is by no means impossible providing you put in the effort.

Below are some valuable tips that, when heeded, will certainly help you to develop better vision.

- *Master basic ball skills*: The less time and energy you expend moving the ball around unnecessarily, the more time and energy you have for monitoring the goings-on around you.
- *Watch soccer games both live and on television, and evaluate the defense*: You will begin to notice that only a small number of plays make up the majority of defensive action. When you see the run-up to these plays, you can then learn to watch out for them in your own games.
- *Occasionally play in different positions*: This will give you a window into the minds of other players on the field, including your opponents.
- *Practice being aware at all times when you are on the field*: Whether you are doing drills, playing a practice game, or in the middle of the most important competition of your soccer career, you should always practice at being aware of the people around you. This should include what they are doing right at that moment, and what they are likely going to be doing next. This will train your mind to hone in on details that matter.

Positional awareness means knowing where you are, where your defenders are, and how your movements are affecting those around you.

You should always work at exploiting and dominating the space you are assigned to.

You should also take note of how the opposing team's defenders move in relation to how you move.

Once you have acquired this awareness, you can plan subtle movements that will pull these defenders out of position, thus opening up holes through which your team can go on to score goals.

Below are some useful approaches for developing positional awareness:

- *Think of soccer as a game of chess:* Every time you move, your opponent will move. Some of these moves are predictable if you take the time to think about the situation.
- *In general, when you move toward a player he will move away, and vice versa:* If you move away from a player, they will likely move toward you. This is especially true if the defensive player in question does not realize what your true intentions are. If you do not have the ball but look as though you expect to receive it shortly, even though you don't, then you can lure the opponent who's marking you away from the action by your misleading moves.

Picture the following situation: A midfielder is moving the ball toward the forward line, yet no one is really in place to receive it yet.

You know from your superior vision of the game that the midfielder will likely pass the ball to a certain player.

However, you can see that a nearby opponent will probably try to interfere with this pass once it happens.

Using this knowledge, you inch ever closer to the defensive player, who without even realizing it starts to move slightly away. This subtle yet smart action then clears the field for the pass.

This is just one basic, everyday situation where you will be using vision and positional awareness to clear the path for more victories.

Using your head to score more goals

A good striker scores a lot of goals from balls that are crossed in from the wings. However, it takes a truly awesome player to score goals from heading balls crossed in from this part of the field. When it comes to strikers in soccer, the difference between being average and being exceptional lies in their ability to get up in the air and get a head on that ball.

Heading the ball into the goal has two distinct advantages. First, it saves you the step of dropping the ball to the ground before shooting, and second, heading decreases the chance of opponents taking possession of the ball.

Because people tend to pause to watch an aerial ball, being able to head it into the goal can quite often catch the goalie and other defenders completely off guard.

Like all soccer moves, heading requires skill and technique if it's to be mastered well.

Listed below are the four most common ways of heading the ball, along with the situations where they are most appropriate:

- *The standard header.* This is the basic, all-purpose header that is used by every soccer player from preschool kids up to the professionals. To achieve this style of heading, start by leaning your head slightly forward while bending your knees. When the ball approaches, you then come upward with your whole body and strike the ball with your upper forehead. It's obviously better to master this header before you take on any of the others.

- *The flick header.* This is one of the most common headers used to score goals, often resulting in a fast moving and often hard to follow ball. This is different from a standard header because you are hitting the ball with the back of your head. The simplest way to do this is to bend your knees slightly and arch your back. You then straighten your knees as the ball makes contact. If the back of your head is aimed squarely at the goal, that will be where the ball heads. This is a great incognito move that will surprise and dismay your opponents at the same time.

- *The glancing header.* Like the flick header, the glancing header can be performed without a lot of obvious preparation. This allows you to sneak the ball in through the goal posts. The glancing header has an advantage over the flick header because it allows you to aim. To perform this header successfully, you need to turn your head toward the place you want the ball to end up and then head it in that direction.
- *The diving header.* The diving header is different from the others because you dive for the ball as you are heading it. It is a tricky move that is much more difficult to perform in reality than it sounds. The best way to practice the diving header is to keep your body elongated with your arms stretched out (keeping the arms out protects your face from hitting the ground). The best way to learn this type of header is to practice diving before adding in the heading part.

As with all soccer skills, these heading techniques must be repeated over and over before they can be truly mastered. It will take some time to get comfortable using them during intense games, so be patient, and remain persistent in your efforts to perform them with skill and accuracy.

In the position of striker, no single skill can make as big a difference as learning how to head the ball into the goal. With this ability in your skills arsenal, you can become the awesome striker you always hoped to be, turning crosses and corner kicks into the impressive goals your team needs for victory.

5 Deep-lying forward (SS) – The All-rounder

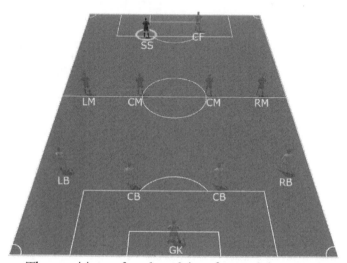

The position of a deep-lying forward is one that varies from region to region, and even from team to team.

Although one of the oldest positions in the game of soccer, it has actually had a variety of names over time, such as second striker, deep-lying playmaker, and deep-lying center.

It has had almost as many different roles on the field as it has had names too.

That said, there are a few key commonalities that all successful deep-lying forwards share.

What is a deep-lying forward?

The first step to understanding this position is to know exactly where a deep-lying forward is positioned on the field.

As the name suggests, these players operate between the midfield and the offensive third of the field.

If you are a deep-lying forward, you will be playing not as a midfielder or as a forward, but as a blend of the two.

Your main job will be to create scoring opportunities for your offense and, at various other times, to attack as well. This contrast of duties has led many Italian teams to call this player the "three-quarters".

It takes a special person to be a deep-lying forward. They must be versatile and have all the strengths of both centre midfielders and strikers.

They must be adept at multitasking and able to judge where they can be of most benefit to their team at any given time.

Essential skills

Because you will be a blend of midfielder and forward, you will need to possess the accurate ball skills that both players exhibit.

Heading skills are also important as you will be stopping many airborne soccer balls in your role.

Although you are not your team's main goal scorer, you are still expected to take advantage of every scoring opportunity that comes your way.

This means that kicking and shooting skills are important as well.

Passing is another very important skill for a deep-lying forward.

If you don't possess very good passing abilities, then you will almost certainly fail in this position.

Essential personality traits

Teamwork is not an option but an absolute must-do. The deep-lying forward usually does not function as a leader on the team but he's very much a team player.

Your physical position on the field can make it difficult to keep close tabs on other players. Therefore, you will mainly be carrying out plans devised by others, and opening channels for them to succeed with their moves.

Fearless determination in duels will also help you when faced with an intimidating defensive line.

You must also be able to perform well without the applause and encouragement that other forwards tend to enjoy.

You are the foundation of the offense and as such will not often get the accolades you deserve.

Another essential personality trait is the ability to stay focused, even when there is constant distraction going on all around you.

You will spend most of the game in the middle of the intense action, but you must be able to see through the chaos and know what you can do to best assist your team.

Benefits and Drawbacks

This is a great position for anyone who wants to be in the heart of the action. You will always be surrounded by other players and plenty of commotion.

As stated previously, one potential drawback to this position is that it's a supporting role which offers little in the way of glory.

However, this is an obvious benefit for players who like to avoid the limelight, as some invariably do.

The other drawback is that you will have such a diverse range of duties that it will be difficult at times to know exactly where you should be or what you should be doing.

For some, this is a welcome challenge, for others it's an impossible demand.

Therefore, this is a role where you must relish in the chaos and always be searching for your next move, the place where you will be of most use to the team at any given time.

Should you play as deep-lying forward?

Many players have had a lot of success playing in this position, and you can be the next if you have the right combination of personality traits and skills, along with a willingness to give the job the attention and practice it demands.

All you need are solid basic soccer skills, a sense of teamwork, and a willingness to play in the background rather than in the spotlight.

Players who excel in this position are rare, so mastering it can give your team a real advantage.

The most important skills

If you are a deep-lying forward, then you will definitely have your work cut out for you in every game.

Your specific role is to create attacks as well as to take shots from outside the penalty box.

More generally, you are also expected to create scoring opportunities for the other forwards and back up your offensive team whenever they need your assistance.

If you are wondering whether you have what it takes to play this important role on your team, then continue reading the remainder of this chapter and you will have a much better idea.

Although most of the necessary skills for this position are easy to practice, the truly great players are few and far between.

The list below shows the main requirements needed for anyone hoping to step into the boots of a deep-lying forward.

- *Ball handling skills*: You will be handling the ball under pressure and while being marked by one or more opponents in what can be a highly stressed atmosphere. You will need to move the ball decisively and accurately, without getting flustered. The only way to show composure while executing moves in strained conditions is to practice over and over in calmer settings as you prepare for the real competitions.

- *First touch on the ball*: You'll be using your first-touch skills often because the ball spends a lot of time in your area. You need to know how to receive the ball smoothly and play it immediately. First-touch skills can truly set a deep-lying forward apart from the other players.

- *Shooting with accuracy*: Because you are stationed very near to the goal, you will have plenty of opportunities to shoot. Obviously the quicker and more accurate you are, the more goals you will score.

- *Knowing when to pass and who to pass to*: Sometimes you're not in a position to take the shot when you have the ball in your possession. In these situations, you can then turn your disadvantage into the team's benefit if another player is available, that is providing you know what his options are and can get the ball over to him quickly and accurately.
- *Don't underestimate aggression*: A healthy dose of aggression is an asset in the game of soccer, but it can be especially advantageous in the position of deep-lying forward. Never hold back when protecting your space, your ball, or your chance to shoot.
- *Superior shielding skills*: As with all forward positions, you will find that the opposing team's defensive players are constantly marking you. Having superior shielding skills, including being able to put yourself squarely between opponents and the ball, will prevent many interceptions.
- *Confidence*: As a deep-lying forward, you will have to think fast and make decisions without hesitation. Confidence is definitely a must have asset when it comes to this position. Without it, you will miss too many windows of opportunity while contemplating what to do next.

The deep-lying forward is the link between midfielders and strikers. He holds the key to getting the ball into the goal.

This is why technical skills are absolutely crucial for anyone playing in this position.

It's important to know what your most essential skills are, and then practice them until they become second nature to you.

Do this and you will experience a long string of wins and a team that appreciates you for your valued contribution to the side.

Pay attention, plan and predict

A deep-lying forward has a lot to think about and a lot to do. It's easy to wear yourself out in this position if you lose your focus and run yourself ragged.

There will also be times when you never really feel like you're accomplishing anything.

The main reason for this is because playing as a deep-lying forward means serving so many roles.

With all that responsibility to shoulder, there's always a risk of becoming overwhelmed and spreading yourself too thin.

However, nothing needs to be as bad as it seems.

Deep-lying forwards can gain the focus they need to perform effectively providing they stay ever mindful of the following three-step formula: one, pay attention to the game, two, predict the opponent's next move, and three, make a plan to lead your team to a score.

When the role is kept within this basic concept, and the mind is not allowed to stray from it, then you will find that your game has a lot more structure, form, and overall success.

You may think that this is easier said than done, but it's really not so hard to adhere to once practiced. After all, most of the best plans are uncomplicated in their basic form.

People often turn simple concepts into unnecessarily complicated ordeals by too much overthinking, so keep things simple and you will be just fine.

Below is a short guide that will help you implement this three-step plan into your own style of play:

- *Pay attention around you:* Take a look around at your opponents. Don't just observe obvious signs like where they are looking or their facial expression. You can often distinguish important actions from less noticeable movements. Get used to watching the players' feet and bodies rather than their faces. It's harder to fake intentions using body language than it is to fake with facial expressions. Alternately, you can watch for diagonal movements on the field. These often indicate that opponents are moving into some sort of play formation. Whatever you decide to watch for, the most important thing is that you are forever looking and learning how to read player's intentions. If you start to pay close attention on a regular basis you will get to notice patterns and learn when the time is right to move proactively.

- *Predict your opponent's next move*: This is where a wealth of practice and real life experience will be of huge benefit to you. When it comes to the learning strategy, start by studying matches, both televised and by attending live games. Second is firsthand experience, and this is only something that can come from playing lots of games and attending plenty of practice sessions. It is one thing trying to predict a player's next move from a spectator's perspective, but it is something quite different when you're in the thick of an intense game. Both approaches are necessary in order to build up this essential skill. The sooner you start learning how to predict player's next moves on the field, the quicker you will become good at it. Once you have determined what play is about to be executed, you can then draw on your bank of acquired information and make an informed decision on what actions to take next.

- *Create a plan*: Once you know what your opponent is thinking and how they intend to proceed, or have at least narrowed it down to a few possibilities, then you can plan how to respond for the best effect. If your team has the ball already, you can use what you know to counter your opponent's attempts to intercept that ball or foil whatever plan they were hoping to use to prevent you from scoring. If you think the opposing team is preparing to make a pass, then you need to position yourself so that a pass is not possible. If you foresee a move up the field, close down any holes that will make that movement easier. The key here is to use the information you have concluded to close down your opponent's options and force them to turn the ball back over to your side.

This might all sound a little difficult, impossible even, but it's not anywhere near as hard as it appears in print.

Like so many other skills, it takes a lot longer to read and comprehend the steps necessary to learn a thing than it does to actually put it into action, which is usually nanoseconds, that's once you have mastered the skill of course.

Become mindful of the above steps and start working on them right away.

You will soon get to learn what to look out for and how to act based on both your observations and ever-developing intuition.

This is how the world's best deep-lying forwards play at every single game, and it's the reason they are so good in the position.

Remember to keep things simple. All these steps basically boil down to is intuition, constantly developing that intuition, and putting it to good use.

Intuition is one skill that every soccer player can use to his benefit, but it is especially important in the role of the deep-lying forward.

It's a tough job but hey, someone has to do it. If you hope to become the team's deep-lying forward, that "someone" will be you. Are you ready for the challenge?

The all-purpose player

Although many describe this position as a type of director for their team's attack, in reality they often play in a variety of roles, including forwards and as midfield extras.

If you are a deep-lying forward you may struggle occasionally with knowing exactly what to do at any given time.

The answer for most players in this position is to simply adapt yourself so that you meet the specific needs of your teammates at that particular moment in time.

Below are a few situations that illustrate the most useful place for you to be in each of these circumstances.

- *When the ball is coming up the field, you should work on making yourself open for it, or create an opening for another teammate*: This will make it easier for the midfield to pass the ball on without interference from the other side, and consequently bring you much closer to the opponent's goal area.
- *When a cross is coming your way, you should try to shoot or head the ball into the goal*: If a shot at the goal is not possible, your next option should be to clear the way for one of your teammates to take the necessary action. This could either be by holding back the defense or simply staying out of the way.
- *When a forward on your team has the ball, your thinking should shift from creating openings for passes to creating openings for shooting*: Whether you are holding off the opposing defense, creating a distraction, or getting ready to receive the ball, your aim in this situation should be an attempt at scoring or creating a scoring opportunity for a teammate.

- *After a shot has been taken, a deep-lying forward can support the team by waiting near the goal box to finish if necessary.* Even if a goalie intercepts the ball, the chances of a score may still be high. Don't forget, just because the keeper saves the ball, that doesn't always mean he's got control of it. So providing you are in place and ready to take another shot, should the ball come back into play, then anything can still happen. A team that knows how to finish well can make up to twice as many goals as one that doesn't pursue the ball after the first attempt to score.

- *When the opposing side retakes the ball, you can help your team best by closing down the opponent's options for getting closer to your own goal area.* Whether you act by eliminating holes in the field or by aggressively pursuing the ball, your job now is to stop the opponents advance in whatever way you can.

- *When your team is losing the will to continue, you can play a huge role in lifting spirits, especially with the morale of the forward line.* You can come up with a play that will save the day and lead your team to victory, or merely offer encouragement that the players need to survive and thrive in a difficult game. Moods and attitude can be infectious, so use a positive approach to help inject a little optimism back into your side.

These suggestions are not written in stone, they are merely guidelines to help you decide where you can do the most good in various situations.

If you ask a soccer expert about the particular talents of a deep-lying forward, creativity and ball skills are sure to come up as the top must-have qualities.

The need for these skills arises from the need to adapt to the needs of the team.

When you learn to adjust your play to each unique situation, your forward line will become truly unstoppable.

Ending...

My final piece of advice to you is this: If you have dreams do not give up on them, not even if someone you look up to says you can't do a thing.

Remember to always, always, always believe in yourself, especially when stuff doesn't seem to be going according to plan, in fact, especially when stuff doesn't seem to be going according to plan.

Remember too, there cannot be any progress without some failure and setbacks along the way, there just can't be, and so be mindful of this whenever things get tough. If you don't believe in yourself then those who you need for encouragement and support won't be able to believe in you either.

Be mindful of the fact that there is only one real failure in this life of ours and that is the failure to try. I sincerely wish you the very best in all your endeavors to succeed.

Mirsad Hasic